Hostilities Only

David Buckle

with
Jan Greenough

Hostilities Only

David Buckle

with
Jan Greenough

First published in 1999 by Robert Dugdale, Oxford
and distributed from
26 Norham Road
Oxford
OX2 6SF

© 1999 David Buckle and Jan Greenough

ISBN 0 946976 08 2

Contents

Acknowledgements

To Beryl, to whom I owe so much, and can never repay for all her tolerance and understanding of such a difficult husband. And to my two sons, Alan and Peter, for making me so proud of them.

I should also like to record my grateful thanks to Hugo Brunner, Lord Lieutenant of Oxfordshire, for all his support and encouragement througout this project.

The excerpt from *Back from the Brink* by Michael Edwardes is reproduced by kind permission of HarperCollins Publishers.

1. Home from Home

I was three years old, and I was frightened. Someone tall was holding my hand and trying to reassure me, saying that everything was going to be all right. We were in a strange house, opening a dark wood-panelled door, going into a gloomy room. Adults were talking over my head. I leaned against a rough wooden bench and saw that on the table in front of me, on a level with my eyes, were some chipped and battered enamel mugs.

Why the image of those mugs should be so clear I do not know. I had been delivered to the place that was to be my home, and I have no memory at all before that: no mother or father, no house, no familiar bed or toy that I must have known for three years had etched itself into my mind. All that remains after seventy years is the small, dark room, the fear, and the chipped enamel mugs.

It was many years before I began even to try to piece together the story of my life, and in the end it proved impossible. The only person who could have known the facts was my Guardian, whom I (and all the other children) called 'Auntie', and it was evidently part of her stock-in-trade that children should not be able to trace their parentage. The children's home was run by her as a private business, and certainly was not registered with the local authorities in any sense which we would recognise today. I suspect that many of the children in her care were illegitimate, including me, and that she took them in exchange for large sums of money to relieve middle-class and upper-class families of embarrassment. She once hinted to me – but only hinted – that my father was a furrier in the City of London, and so he would have been a wealthy man. If I was born from some irregular liaison with a maid in his home (for all well-to-do homes had several servants in those days) then it is quite likely that I would be disposed of as soon as was practical.

I have no birth certificate. Miss Butler, my Guardian, always told me, 'If anyone ever asks you about your parents, tell them that your father and mother died in a car crash.' However, much later, when I was evacuated to Oxfordshire, the last words she said to me as I was getting on the train were, 'David, if ever you are in a very serious situation, remember that your name is not Buckle, but Clarke – with an e.' Quite what the serious situation might be, and how this snippet of information might help, she did not explain, and there was no time to question her; after the war I visited her in an attempt to find out more, but she still refused to tell me anything. I suppose that if my father really did want to get me out of his life completely, all he had to do was to ask Miss Butler to give me a different surname. Depriving a child of his parents' names effectively deprives him of access to any records. In later life I have often thought that all those employers who kept calling me a bastard didn't know how near the truth they were!

The children's home was a large semi-detached house in Mitcham in south London, and I must have been among the first arrivals, for I was always the eldest child in the home. As the numbers increased, the Mitcham house became too small, and Miss Butler transferred her enterprise to Ringstead Road in Sutton. With us went the other two members of the household: Auntie Rosie, the cook, and Brian Butler. Quite what relationship Brian bore to Auntie I never knew – perhaps a nephew or even a son. He was a little older than me, and lived with us but under quite a different regime. He had a room of his own, better clothes, and better food; I often served him breakfast in bed. In my eyes he was a spoilt fat brat, enjoying luxuries such as chocolate which we never got the chance to taste.

My Guardian was an austere woman, tall and slim with grey hair. She always wore a blue uniform, rather like a hospital matron, which emphasised the formal relationship she had with her charges. She was softly spoken but her words were always severe: she never expressed any affection, verbal or physical, to the children in her care. Auntie Rosie was a softer character, short and dumpy, who loved children and was kinder to us: she would feed us scraps when we were helping in the kitchen.

By the time we moved I was old enough (maybe five or six) to help in the house, and I was given a series of tasks, scrubbing floors, helping in the kitchen, or raking grass and leaves in the garden. There were a couple of cleaning ladies who came in each day, but the home was run as cheaply as possible and there were always extra jobs for me. This was when the beatings started: I suppose I was too small to do any of these things particularly well, and I was always punished for anything that was not done properly. I was a normal little boy, so I must sometimes have been naughty and disobedient, but I soon learned what the result would be. Miss Butler would either hit me with a leather strap, or she would hold a book in both hands and bring it down hard on top of my head. I realise that she must sometimes have been driven to distraction by us children, and her irritation was clear. Yet I seldom felt that she had lost her temper when she hit me; rather, it was an act of cold, controlled discipline. Occasionally it was less controlled, and became excessive, but I am sure she would always have justified her actions by saying that she was trying to bring us up as well as she could.

I recall one night in particular, when I went to bed very unhappy, and lay on my back crying. I had been hit several times that day, and my head ached badly. I was rocking my head from side to side for comfort, when I suddenly felt something wet and sticky running down my neck. I put my hand up to feel it, and found my fingers covered in pus. The next morning I told my Guardian that something was wrong with my ear, and she took me to a doctor. He insisted that I must go to the local hospital, and all the while the doctors were treating me, Miss Butler was telling them how worried she was about me.

'Poor David,' she kept saying, 'We can't think how this could have happened. We love him so much, and we're so worried about him.'

I looked up at her in astonishment: she had certainly never told me that she loved me before! I was fully aware that it was her beatings that had caused the pain in my head, but I was much too frightened of her to say anything. It would never have occurred to me that I could have told anyone or complained of the way I was treated: the home was my only home, and I knew nothing else. But I did understand quite clearly that she wasn't behaving normally, that she was telling lies, and that she was doing so for the benefit of the doctors.

I was duly discharged, and went home to my usual routine; the beatings continued as before. Eventually I was taken into hospital again with a serious recurrence of the same mastoid trouble, and this time it required an operation to remove part of the bone (I still have quite a deep hole behind my left ear). It seems curious, in these days of hospital porters, trolleys and sterile gowns, to think that I walked alone into the operating theatre and was told by the anaesthetist to 'hop up onto that table'. Laid out on a table at the side were all the surgical instruments needed for the operation, and pretty terrifying they looked to a small boy.

'Lie down,' said the anaesthetist, and I did so. 'Now,' he continued, 'I'm going to put this mask over your face, and I'm going to drop some chloroform onto the wool. It may give you a headache, but you'll soon go to sleep and you won't know any more about it. Now I want you to count backwards from ten to one.' I remember seeing him bending over me with the bottle in his hand, shaking the drops of chloroform onto the woollen mask over my mouth and nose. My head began to thump heavily, and I counted down as far as seven before the blackness came up and swamped me. When I came round I was lying in a cot with my head heavily bandaged, vomiting endlessly into a bowl. My Guardian was standing over me, wailing just as she had done before.

'Oh, my poor David. We just want you to come home safely, we're all so worried about you. I don't like to see you suffer like this.' Even through the haze of anaesthetic, the pain and vomiting, I remember feeling angry with her. She had never shown the slightest consideration for me at home, and all I ever got from her were blows on the head from a book or a strapping. I wished she would go away and leave me alone. I gather that I had come close to death during that mastoid operation.

Although I was too young to give a name to the hypocrisy of my Guardian's affection and concern for me in the hospital, I was nevertheless able to recognise it in some sense. I knew that she had pretended feelings she did not have, to impress the doctors and nurses (though in later life I realised that she may well have been afraid, even in those less wary days, of being charged with assault). I was unable to articulate any of this, but it did affect me. I began to show signs of rebellion and 'awkwardness'; I refused, whenever I thought it was reasonably safe to do so, to toe the line. Of course, there was usually a price to pay.

The main staircase at Ringstead Road was impressive, sweeping up in a spiral out of the large hall. At Christmas Miss Butler always managed to get a fine Christmas tree, which stood in the hall and extended right up the stairwell. Every child would have a stocking tied to the banisters around the tree, and we would come out of our rooms onto the landings to collect the stocking with our name on it. There would be some lights on the tree, and Miss Butler, who was deeply religious, made sure that we sang carols before giving us permission to open the stockings in which Father Christmas had usually provided a balloon, a paper hat and an orange, and perhaps a very small second-hand toy.

The year I was seven I decided that I didn't believe in Father Christmas, and on Christmas Eve I said so. 'Well, David, you're wrong,' said Miss Butler. 'There is a Father Christmas and he will come, you'll see.' The next day we were all called out as usual to collect our stockings, and I noticed that mine was looking rather thin. When we were told to open our gifts, I felt inside and found that it contained nothing but a large chunk of coal!

'What's this?' I asked.

'Well, you said you didn't believe in Father Christmas, so Father Christmas has got his own back on you,' was the reply. 'He's left you a lump of coal, and that's all you're going to get.' In fact in the end I wasn't deprived of everything: later in the day I was given my orange and my present. It was a salutary lesson to me – and one I probably deserved, because Miss Butler clearly went to a great deal of trouble to provide even such meagre offerings for every child in the home.

It was becoming hard, though, to remember to be grateful for every tiny thing, when we were all growing up and becoming aware that other children lived a very different kind of life. It was not only material things we lacked: relationships within the home were neither close nor affectionate. In spite of Miss Butler's protestations in the hospital, she never showed any emotion in her dealings with us, and certainly no love. A more romantic view of our situation might suggest that we children would band together as partners in adversity but the reverse was true: we circled each other warily, watchful in case anyone managed to get more food or clothes than the others. We had never received any affection ourselves, so we had no idea how to offer it; we had no idea how normal relationships worked. We interacted more like enemies than siblings: we fought over everything, especially food. It was a case of the survival of the fittest. You never dared to show any sign of weakness, or you would go to the wall.

There was one girl in particular, called Grace, who was a real rough diamond. She was freckled, fair, and plump, but she was a tough tomboy. I fought her on many occasions, and although we sometimes walked to school together, I would not describe our relationship as anything like a friendship. Yet we kept in touch after we were all evacuated, and we still write to each other. I was glad of this after I married, for I began to feel that my wife Beryl sometimes suspected me of exaggerating stories of life in the home. When we met up with Grace she corroborated my stories and added to them, much to Beryl's surprise.

When I was about eight we moved again.

Miss Butler announced it one morning when we were all together in the sort of assembly she held after breakfast. 'We are going to move to a big country house in Kent,' she said, and of course this was the sign that the home was expanding once more. In Kent we had fifty children in the house, and the whole enterprise was scaled up yet again. The new house stood in about five acres of its own grounds, and was approached up a long drive from the road. At the front was a large, well-kept lawn which was out of bounds to us children, and behind it was a garden, then a second kitchen garden and beyond them, fields full of rabbits. The house itself was a rambling place with over twenty rooms, a cellar which doubled as a boiler room, and an annexe which must once have been the stables, but which now contained small bedrooms.

In many ways life here was much better. For one thing, we all enjoyed being able to roam about freely in the countryside, which was a welcome relief after the town. It lessened some of the stress of being cooped up in the unnatural situation of the children's home. We also discovered, that first autumn, that the hedgerows could supplement our poor diet, and we soon located the best blackberry bushes and did a fair amount of scrumping from local orchards on our way to and from school.

I have no recollection of going to school at all in Mitcham or Sutton, but in Kent I know that I attended Borough Green Elementary School; I think I was seven or eight when I started. We had a half-mile walk to school, along country lanes, and Grace and I used to have to push three of the smallest children in an old pram, because it was too far for them to walk. All of us kept together on the way to school and in the playground, because for the first time we found ourselves allies against the rest of the world. We were known as the Crouch House kids, and we were an easy target for the gangs of local boys. We stood out in our odd assortment of rag-bag clothes.

I remember once being given a pair of girl's boots to wear: old-fashioned ones that laced right up to the knee. I dutifully wore them down the drive, but I was not going to endure the teasing they would earn me at school, so once outside I took them off and hid them in a ditch, and went to school barefoot. When the teacher asked me where my shoes were, I said I didn't have any, as the home could not afford them. This must have been an acceptable reply, for no further questions were asked, and I collected the boots on the way home each afternoon.

Clothes were a constant source of irritation; no one could have been less fashion-conscious than we were, yet it was annoying to wear clothes that were always shabby and seldom fitted properly. On one occasion I was given a white shirt that was almost new, and I was very proud of it. Unfortunately, on that very day I did something to annoy the teacher, and he grabbed me by the shirt to pull me into line, and tore it. I was so angry that I turned round and struck out at him, shouting 'You've torn my shirt!' For that I received five strokes with the cane, in front of my giggling classmates, who loved to see the Crouch House kids in trouble.

I was a poor scholar, well behind my fellow pupils at this stage and unable to read or write properly. The only time I recall receiving any kind of praise was when a visitor came to give us a talk about the evils of drink, and we were asked to write about it afterwards. I submitted a poorly written piece, but I must have understood his message, because I was given a prize! I was often absent from school, either because there was work to be done at the home, or simply because I played truant. My hearing was poor in one ear, a legacy of those early illnesses, and I had developed a severe stammer, so I found it hard to make myself understood. It was not a recipe for academic success.

My housework duties continued in the new home, though the tasks seemed larger in proportion to the larger scale of the house. It had long stone passageways, and one of my regular jobs was to scrub these with soapy water. I also had to take a tray of tea and bread and butter to my

Guardian every afternoon in her study, and return it to the kitchen when she had finished. If ever there was any bread and butter left, I would cram it into my mouth as soon as I was outside the door – it left me with a tremendous liking for butter which has lasted all my life. When I got to the kitchen Auntie Rosie would say, 'Did she leave anything on the plate?'

'Yes,' I replied.

'Well, where's it gone?'

'I've eaten it.'

'Oh, well done,' she would say.

In Kent I realised that my Guardian no longer beat me for any minor infringements of her demands. This was not because I was behaving better, but rather because I think she was genuinely afraid of harming me, after the two episodes in hospital. Instead, she had thought up a different punishment which would leave no apparent physical damage.

If I failed to work properly or did anything else to annoy her, she would say, 'Right, it's the cellar for you.'

This meant that I would be locked alone in the cellar for up to two days; food and drink would be brought down to me, but I had to stay there and stoke the coal boiler which heated the water for the house. There were no windows, of course, not even a grating to the ground outside, but there was an electric light which I could switch on and off. There was a pile of sacks for bedding, but I didn't get much sleep: it was dark and lonely, and I was frightened of the rats.

It was not a regular punishment – I don't suppose I was put down there more than two or three times – but it was a terrifying experience, and the threat of it certainly ensured that I was very careful about my behaviour. Outwardly I became more obedient and submissive; inwardly I raged at my helplessness and resented the power that could do that to me.

With hindsight, viewed from this end of the century, such treatment seems unbelievably brutal; how common it could have been in 1930 I have no idea. This woman was not a cynical exploiter of child labour, nor a sadistic torturer; she was a religious, churchgoing woman, well thought of in the local community who supported with gifts and donations her efforts to look after children who had nowhere else to go. Few of her friends could have had any idea of our treatment behind the closed doors of the home – and yet thanks to her we were not starving, homeless, nor exploited in any worse ways: for in spite of all the physical abuse I suffered in my childhood I never once was abused sexually, nor touched in any way inappropriately by anyone.

Miss Butler was an ardent supporter of the church. Her favourite saying, after 'Manners maketh man' was 'Cleanliness is next to godliness', and she set great store by godliness. On Empire Day, when we were all given a little Union Flag to wave, the vicar came to listen to us singing 'Rule Britannia'. That was how he discovered that I had a tuneful treble voice, and decided that he could do with my help in the church choir. It was no use my protesting that I didn't want to go to church; Miss Butler thought that helping the vicar might be even more efficacious than cleanliness in improving me. My friend Mohan Williams, whose father was a senior official in the Indian Embassy, had to come too, and together we spent most of our Sundays in church. We sang at the early communion, the main morning service, the children's afternoon service, and evensong. It probably put me off church for life. As the church was one and a half miles away in the village of Plaxtall, it was too far for us to come home at midday, so we took a sandwich lunch and ate it among the pews.

Sundays were stultifyingly boring, so it was not surprising that eventually we got up to mischief. One lunchtime, left alone in the church, we climbed up into the bell tower and started tolling the bells as though for a funeral. I looked out through the thin slit windows and saw the vicar hurrying out of his house and along the path to the church. He threw us out and told Miss Butler that he did not want to see us in church again. If we had known what would happen we would have rung the bells weeks before!

Around this time there was a diphtheria epidemic, which inevitably affected some of the children in the home, as we were less than robust and had little resistance to infections. Miss Butler called us all together after breakfast for one of her announcements.

'Some of the children in the annexe are ill,' she said, 'and they will be taken away to the hospital soon.' Grace and I slept in rooms in the annexe but we had been lucky enough to escape infection. We kept looking out for the ambulance which would take them away, but it never came. Instead, Miss Butler told us that they had died, and that they would be taken away in coffins instead. I was terrified on two counts: firstly that I might catch diphtheria, too, since I slept in the same building, and secondly, that I might see someone dead. I remember the coffins arriving and being laid on the grass outside the annexe, but I don't recall seeing the children carried out.

The next day my Guardian called me, Grace, and two of the other older children together.

'These rooms have got to be fumigated before anyone else can use them,' she said. 'Because the children died in there, the rooms have to be made safe. The man will come this afternoon with the fumigating equipment, but I want you to go in and prepare the rooms for him.'

It was a complicated business. The beds and chairs had to be pulled away from the wall, and all the bedding had to be stripped off the beds and spread out in a single layer on the floor, so that it would be exposed to the fumes. Then we applied waxed tape around the edges of all the windows, to seal them. When the man arrived we hung about in the corridor to watch him. He went into the first room with a large canister in his hand, ripped back a stopper from the top of it, and placed it in the middle of the floor. Then he rushed back outside, closed the door, locked it, and began to put masking tape all around the edge of the door. The he turned round and saw us.

'Listen, you children,' he said. 'You mustn't go in there for at least two days, it isn't safe. Understand? Now, off you go, and stay well away.'

Two days later Miss Butler sent for us again. 'You can finish doing the rooms now,' she said. 'Take all the tape off the doors and windows and open them to air the rooms. Then take everything out and scrub the room thoroughly. I want it all perfectly clean.'

This was all routine procedure for fumigating rooms in those days; the only difference was that it was not usually done by nine-year-olds.

Exactly on what financial basis the house was run I never inquired, even when I returned to visit my Guardian after the war. I imagine that some children were supported by relations who paid money at intervals to Miss Butler; others probably came with a lump sum and nothing more. She must have struggled at times to feed and clothe us all, and although she, Auntie Rosie and Brian never went hungry, none of them could have made a particularly good living out of us. The tiny children had nowhere else to go, but as we grew older, other possibilities began to present themselves, particularly for those of us who could work and be of some help around the house.

At the front of Crouch House was an imposing drive sweeping around the circular lawn, which I called 'the Forbidden Lawn' because it was strictly out of bounds to us children. One day Miss Butler sent for me.

'David,' she said, 'today you are going to have a bath and some clean clothes. After that, I want you to go and stand outside on the front lawn.'

When I asked why, she replied, 'Don't ask questions, just get on and do as you're told.'

I duly had my bath, and put on the clothes laid out for me: a white shirt, short trousers, and a grey jacket; they were in considerably better condition than anything I usually had to wear. Then I went out to wait on the lawn.

After a while a chauffeur-driven car arrived: I could see the driver's peaked cap as it passed me. It stopped in front of the house, and a man got out; Miss Butler came out to meet him, and they chatted as they walked across the grass.

I was rather bored with waiting outside all alone, so as they came up to me I thought I would join in the conversation.

'I guessed someone was coming to see me today,' I interrupted brightly, 'because I've had a bath and I've got these nice new clothes on.' The man walked away, and as soon as he had gone, Miss Butler took my trousers down and gave me a good thrashing with the belt. She was furious.

'That's for speaking to that man and telling him you'd had a bath,' she said. 'You are not to speak to people like that, and tell them things.'

I was told to stand on the lawn two or three times after that, but I was always careful not to speak out of turn. Once two cars arrived together, and a man came up and started pinching my cheek (I was rather a thin and scrawny child). 'No, I don't want him,' he said, and left.

I suppose other children had their turns at being paraded in this way, but we didn't think much about it; it was just one of the many inexplicable instructions we were given from time to time. It was only when I visited my Guardian after the war as an adult, in an attempt to find out more about my childhood, that I thought to ask her what had been going on.

'David,' she replied, 'I have to tell you that running that house with all those children was so expensive, that sometimes I had to sell children to raise extra money. I'm afraid that much as I loved you I had to try to sell you – but no one would buy you. Those two men insisted on arguing about the money, and in the end neither of them would give me enough.'

In effect, I had been standing in an auction ring!

I found this an astonishing piece of information, but it confirmed something else I remembered from around the same time. One day I was told that Auntie Rosie was going to take me to London. Since we never went on outings or pleasure trips this was very exciting, and once again I was bathed and dressed up in some decent clothes. We went by train from Borough Green Station, but the best part of the journey for me was crossing London in a tram, and watching the driver pulling all the levers at the front.

We arrived at a huge and grimy building in a busy London street: it was Australia House. We were interviewed by a man with a stack of papers in front of him and at the end he stood up and said to Auntie Rosie, 'I'm afraid I don't think he will be suitable,' and home we went.

I discovered afterwards that my Guardian had tried to place me in one of the schemes run at the time, to populate the Empire with British children – it may have been 'British Boys for British Farms'. When I was rejected by Australia House she tried offering me to British Columbia and Canada, but I was never accepted, and so I had to stay at the home. It was hardly surprising; I was a very puny boy with thin arms and legs, nervous, almost illiterate, and with a bad stammer. I was not much of a bargain for anyone looking for a hard-working youngster to help on a farm. I consider this to be a blessing, and certainly a narrow escape: evidence which has come to light in recent years has shown that many of the children who did go abroad on those schemes were treated like slaves and suffered terribly.

I have no idea how many children she did succeed in placing in this way, or indeed how many she 'sold' to individuals; relationships were vague within the home and I can recollect only a few names and faces from those days. I suppose we took it for granted that from time to time children left the home or were placed elsewhere; it never occurred to us to wonder where they had gone.

Life in the home was not one of unmitigated misery; these were the years of the Depression, and many children who lived in families probably had very little more in material terms than we did. I still feel that the loss of any emotional life, and the lack of any family structure, was probably one of our most severe deprivations. The regime was cold and unloving, and I often wonder whether that frigid but entirely female household affected my attitude to women; I had very little idea of how to express affection. However, I was observant and adventurous, and I soon learned that there were other ways to live.

In Kent we were living in what was known as 'the garden of England' and in the summer months the whole area was invaded with casual labour, as East Enders from London and gypsies came 'hopping' – picking the hops for the breweries – and fruit picking. They would build rough shelters out of wood and corrugated iron, or use makeshift tents, and the gypsies often had proper old-fashioned painted caravans. They were a cheerful, rough and ready crowd, single people and whole extended families, and they were always willing to welcome an extra face around the fire, or hand out an extra plate of food. In the evenings after the day's work was done, they would sing music-hall songs round the fire, and children would fall asleep on any friendly lap and be settled down in a corner somewhere.

I found the whole scene irresistible, and the casual welcome I received when I wandered into their camp made me feel that I belonged. These were poor people: my shabby clothes did not stand out here, and if I was willing to do a day's work with them I was accepted as having earned a share of whatever food was going – usually something better than I was used to. So in summer I would run away from the home on a regular basis, sometimes playing truant from school, but more often at weekends when the home routine was such that I was less likely to be missed. I was always picked up by the local policeman, who knew where to find me, but usually not until Sunday evening, by which time I had had a good taste of a kind of family life. It made the cold charity of the children's home seem even less attractive.

I got a look at other ways of living, too. In the village lived a well-to-do family called the Keith-Lucases, and Mrs Keith-Lucas, who was a widow, let me go to her house in the summer to help cut the grass. In payment I was given a glass of orange juice and some biscuits. I was never allowed into the house, though; if it started to rain, I had to shelter in the tool-shed.

The elder son, Alan, was in his early twenties, and he owned a vintage car with a dickey seat at the back. He would sometimes give us rides, or take three or four of us out into the countryside, to play in

Ashdown Forest; it was a real treat for us to go sweeping down the road in this open car, singing at the tops of our voices. When we got there, we would play on a wire strung across a large pond, a sort of aerial runway, and we often got rather wet and muddy in the process.

I am quite sure that Alan had no other motive in these trips than to brighten up our lives a little; he was a kind man and he knew something about how grim the children's home was. He certainly wasn't either a homosexual or a paedophile. However, one day he got into trouble with my Guardian and we never saw him again.

We had come back from an afternoon in the forest and we were all grubby and covered in mud. Miss Butler was annoyed at our appearance and said, 'You're all filthy! Go up and get into the bath!' Alan meekly trailed upstairs with us, ran a bath full of water, undressed and got into the bath with us. I suppose he was used to communal baths after rugby at school – he certainly never thought anything of it, and he wasn't paying any attention to us. I was only surprised because it was the first time in my life I had seen an adult naked, with pubic hair, so I mentally marked that down as another fact learned.

Then the door opened and Miss Butler walked in, and she was absolutely horrified.

'Alan!' she cried. 'What on earth do you think you're doing? Naked with all these children! Get out at once!'

She ordered him out of the house and he was never allowed back. I still maintain that it was a perfectly innocent situation, and that while he may have been either rather libertarian in his behaviour or possibly merely naive, that he never did or said anything that made us uncomfortable. The only way in which he differed from the other adults of our acquaintance was that he treated us with a cheerful, easy-going kindliness which we were unused to.

We missed Alan's visits and the trips into the forest, and life settled down once again into the humdrum hardship of school and housework. Interestingly, I have recently been shown a manuscript copy of Alan Keith-Lucas's memoirs, in which he mentions Crouch House as an 'orphanage' where the school-age children 'were left pretty much to themselves'. He also says that he went to be with the children two or three times a week after school was over for the day, and that he once took charge for a month 'when the lady who ran it was ill and the staff, of retarded local women from a local institution, had all run away.' I have no clear recollection of such a staff, but I suppose that, as a child, I understood very little of how the home was actually run.

By 1938 the number of children in the house had gone down to about twenty – perhaps through Miss Butler's efforts to populate the Colonies – and Crouch House had become too large for us. We moved back into a town, this time to Ramsgate.

2. The World of Work

When we moved to Ramsgate in 1938 I was very excited at the prospect of living at the seaside. The new house at 21 Vale Square was much smaller than the one at Crouch, for there were only fifteen or twenty children living with us now; Grace had been placed with a foster family, and we wrote to each other occasionally. The house was a narrow, five-storey building on the corner, opposite the church. Brian Butler had what was in the children's eyes the best bedroom on the top floor, opening onto the flat roof. During the summer, if we had been good, Brian would allow a select group of us to go out onto the roof from his room, to watch the Friday night firework display which the town put on to entertain the visitors.

Most of the other children were enrolled in the local school, but Miss Butler told me that I would not be going there.

'It's hardly worth your starting school, David,' she said. 'You'll be fourteen in a few months, and then you can leave and get a job. You just carry on helping around the house until then.'

So while the others went off to school every day, I was left at home sweeping five flights of stairs and washing up. I wasn't too worried: school had never held many attractions for me, though I missed being with others of my own age. Quite soon, however, my Guardian found me a job at a builder's merchants. I was thirteen and a half.

The firm, Dunn & Co, was in Broadstairs, which meant that I had quite a long cycle ride to work every morning. I was employed as an office boy, but I was extremely bad at it. No one had thought to mention to Miss Butler that my tasks would include writing out slips for various items to be loaded onto trucks for delivery, and taking down messages from customers. Since I could hardly read or write, I produced illegible slips bearing the wrong information; because my arithmetic wasn't much better, I couldn't get the quantities right. I got the sack after five or six weeks, and was out of work again, still under fourteen!

Miss Butler must have despaired of getting rid of me, but it was clear that there was one job at which I had lots of experience, and at which she could vouch for my efficiency: housework. Years of being beaten whenever I skimped a task meant that I could be relied on to sweep, dust, polish and wash up with exemplary thoroughness. As ever, my Guardian had made contact with the local church, in this case conveniently situated in the same square as our house, and invited the vicar to visit us. As luck would have it, the vicar was looking for a new houseboy, so I packed my few clothes and moved out of the children's home for the first time in my life – just across the road to the vicarage. It was the perfect solution to Miss Butler's problem, and should have been the safest, easiest transition to the world of work. In fact it produced some of the most horrific memories of my young life.

The Revd Townsend lived with his elderly mother and father and a housekeeper. The vicarage was an imposing, double-fronted house with a wide entrance hall and a large garden. I had never been in such a grand house. I slept in a room at the top of the house, and ate my meals with the housekeeper in the kitchen. She was not particularly friendly (I don't suppose a thirteen-year-old boy was her idea of good company, either) but neither was she over-strict. At least she didn't beat me as my Guardian still did, from time to time, though she did insist that every job was done well. One of my tasks was to polish a set of four large embossed brass plates which stood on special stands in the hall; I spent many hours buffing them to a brilliant shine until my arms ached.

I worked six and a half days a week for the princely sum of five shillings. From this 2s 6d was deducted to pay for my keep (I never begrudged this as the food was much better than we had at home). The remainder was subject to fines for misbehaviour or poor work, and as a result I never received more than 1s 6d. I had to get up at 5.30 a.m., and I found this extremely difficult. I was tired after a long day of physical work, and I suppose I was still growing; at any rate, for the first few weeks I was continually fined for getting up late. In the end the housekeeper gave me a second alarm clock, and I devised a system whereby the first rang at 5.20, and the second, placed in a metal biscuit tin to amplify its ringing, went off at 5.30. That roused me sufficiently to get out of bed.

My first job each day was to prepare and take a tray of tea and bread and butter to the vicar in his bedroom. There were strict rules attached to this little ceremony: I had to knock at the door exactly as the church clock was striking six, not a moment before or after; and the bread had to be cut thinly to precisely the right size of slice (the vicar measured it). If I failed either of these requirements I was fined. My final job of the day was to fill hot water bottles and place them in the beds, so I could never go to bed until the family did.

In many ways the vicar was rather like my Guardian, in that he was a harsh man who believed that he was simply doing his Christian duty in giving me a home and a job and teaching me my duty. Indeed, in some ways he was better, because he never used physical violence against me. However, I was treated with a total lack of sympathy. In winter I would be set to clean all the windows in the coldest weather, standing outside on the lawn in my thin jersey and shorts and crying with cold. As I scrubbed the windows of his study, I could look in and see him reading by a roaring fire, with no thought for what was actually his child labourer.

Occasionally he did deign to notice me. Once a week the Women's Institute held their meeting at the vicarage, and I had to answer the door and welcome in all the ladies as they arrived. I found this an embarrassing activity, as they were all very smartly dressed and I was still wearing the shabby second-hand clothes I had been given at the children's home.

'Couldn't I have something different to wear when I answer the door?' I asked. 'I do look scruffy when people come.'

'You're right,' the vicar replied. 'I think we'll have to get you a page-boy outfit.'

So I was duly despatched into the town to be measured for a smart opening-the-door outfit, with shiny buttons.

'And would you like a cap with it, sir?' asked the tailor. I thought a cap would be the last word in fashion, so I ordered that as well, all to be put on the vicar's bill. When the suit arrived I was delighted with it – they were the first new clothes I had ever had in my life, and probably the first that had fitted.

'But you are not to wear that silly cap!' instructed the vicar, so I hid it in my room. At least I had it, and it was mine.

On Sundays we would walk in a solemn procession down the drive and along the road to the church: I was in front, followed by the housekeeper, then Mr and Mrs Townsend, and finally the vicar himself. After lunch I was free for a couple of hours, to go down to the beach which was about five minutes' walk away, or back across the road to the children's home to visit my friends. I had to be back in time for evensong, and afterwards I had to hurry back to the vicarage to lay the table for supper.

At church I would see all the others from the children's home, and once again Mohan and I were made to sing in the choir. Perhaps we remembered our method of extricating ourselves from the unwelcome attentions of the church at Plaxtall, because eventually the vicar threw us out of the choir here, too. This time it was for vandalism at harvest festival: left alone in the church, we threw all the softest tomatoes at the wall, where they landed with a satisfying squelch and made a runny mess on all the stone memorials. I can't say exactly why we did it: it certainly wasn't a plan to get ejected from the choir. It was more a mindless expression of the anger we felt, which was usually kept well below the surface. But the repression of the church services seemed to be a part of the whole emptiness of our cold little lives, and it was immensely satisfying to express our feelings in that antisocial and messy way. I would never condone vandalism, but perhaps I can understand it a little.

On the whole I was not unhappy. Life at the vicarage was very much like life at the home, and I didn't feel that things had changed much. I still worked hard for little or no reward, I was often cold and tired, though seldom hungry, and no one ever showed me any kind of concern or affection. Since I had never known anything else, I could not see how things could be any different. It would not have occurred to me to complain.

However, my worst experience at the vicarage finally made me understand that some things could not be borne, and that it was possible to break out of the circumstances in which I was placed.

Mrs Townsend was an elderly woman – she seemed fantastically old to me, at fourteen – and she had become increasingly frail. Late one winter afternoon the vicar called me and the housekeeper up to his study and informed us that his mother had died. There were several arrangements to be made and he and his father went out shortly afterwards. Then the housekeeper went out for the evening, leaving me alone in the house. Back at Crouch at the time of the diphtheria epidemic one of my worst fears had been that I would have to see a dead body; now I was left alone in the house with one. I sat downstairs in the kitchen for hours, hoping that someone would come home, but in the end I knew I would have to go upstairs to put the hot water bottles in the beds.

I boiled the kettle and filled the bottles, and then crept fearfully up the wide staircase to the first floor where the family's bedrooms were. I was heading for the vicar's room when I glanced over my shoulder and saw that Mrs Townsend's bedroom door had been left open. She had been laid out on the bed with her hands folded on the counterpane. Around the bed were four tall candlesticks, with lit candles casting a flickering light on the still body. It was a scene worthy of a Victorian novel, and it was too eerie for my nervous disposition. I dropped the hot water bottles and ran down the stairs, out of the front door and across the road to the only refuge I knew – the children's home.

I was crying with fear and shaking with tension when I burst into my Guardian's study.

'David, what on earth is the matter?' she cried, and tried to make sense of my incoherent account. When I had finished she regarded me sternly.

'Well, I agree that you can't go back there on your own tonight. You can have a bed here, and I'll go across and tell the housekeeper where you are when she gets home. But tomorrow you must go back, David, and explain your behaviour.'

I found an empty bed in a dormitory and slept an exhausted sleep.

The next morning I crossed the road again and went straight to the vicar's study.

'So, David, why did you run away last night?'

'I was afraid,' I replied.

'Afraid? What was there to be afraid of? You were never afraid of Mrs Townsend when she was alive, were you? So there is no need to be afraid of her now that she is dead.'

'No, sir,' I answered. 'I won't run away again. Shall I go down to the kitchen now?'

'Certainly not,' said the vicar. 'You have to learn not to be afraid of death. The dead cannot hurt us, they have gone to be with Jesus. Come with me.' He grabbed me by the arm and frog-marched me up the stairs to his mother's room. Although the staircase was less frightening in the morning light, the heavy curtains were still closed in the bedroom, and the candles were still burning around the bed. It made the room look darker than ever. I pulled back in the doorway, but the vicar had a grip like steel and he dragged me to the bedside. I turned my head away so that I did not have to look at that lined old face, now relaxed in death. Mr Townsend was furious.

'It's only my mother!' he shouted. 'Look at her! Look at her! I'll show you there's nothing to be afraid of.' Then he grabbed my head in his hand and forced my face down onto hers. 'Kiss her! Then you'll know you shouldn't be afraid! Kiss her!'

I was shaking with revulsion as he pushed my face onto hers – her soft skin was icy cold. Then he let me go and somehow I managed to walk out of the room.

I went straight back to the children's home, and this time my Guardian made no comment as I walked in. She could see that my face was ashen and I was shaking all over. It was some time before I could tell her what had happened.

Mercifully, this time she took my part.

'Please don't make me go back again,' I pleaded.

'No,' she answered, 'you need never go back there. We'll have to find you something else.'

I was surprised but thankful that she had decided to stand up for me against the vicar, who was usually her ally. It was part of the strange relationship I had with her: she always professed great affection for the children in her care, without ever giving us the slightest sign of it. Yet at the crucial moment she supported me, and I was always grateful for that. She also took me back into the home, when by rights I suppose I should have been working and looking after myself. Once again she was faced with the problem of helping me to find work.

This time she was much more successful. She found me a job as an errand boy with an ironmonger's shop in Ramsgate. I had a black 'sit up and beg' bicycle with a huge wicker basket on the front, and on this I happily rode around Ramsgate making deliveries to customers' homes. The men in the shop were cheerful and friendly, and teased the new boy in the time-honoured way, sending me out on rogue errands for a tin of striped paint or to buy three haircuts. But by now I was beginning to have a little self-confidence, and was learning how to look after myself.

On the haircut errand I went off down to the seafront and amused myself for an hour or so on the beach. When I got back to the shop the owner asked me where I had been.

'Well, I went for those haircuts but there was a long queue,' I replied. That got a laugh and a gentle cuff round the ear, and the teasing stopped.

I enjoyed being out in the fresh air for much of the day, after all those years of being confined to the home by housework duties. Occasionally I took my time on deliveries, walking by the sea or just cycling around the town; when questioned I could always say that I had had difficulty finding the delivery address. The shop was open very late in the summer months, and on a Saturday night it was my task to cycle over to Broadstairs once the shop had closed, taking a bag of pairs of scissors to be sharpened. I would wait for them to be dealt with by the grinder, and then cycle back. I often didn't return until after ten o'clock – a long day's work for a fourteen-year-old. But I was growing stronger and fitter, and generally enjoying life.

Ramsgate was a lively place to be, especially during the season when the summer visitors filled the streets and the seafront, and the promenade was lit up with fairy lights at night. It was hard to believe that things would ever be any different. But this was 1939, and even I was aware that the storm clouds of war were gathering. By that summer we had stopped thinking that it would all blow over and were simply waiting for an announcement to be made. On September 3rd Miss Butler gathered all the children together to listen to the radio at eleven o'clock. Like everyone else all around the country, we listened in silence as Neville Chamberlain spoke. We were officially at war with Germany.

During the afternoon I was standing outside the house in the sunshine, when I saw several men in uniform hurrying along the street towards the Territorial Army Headquarters, which was just around the corner.

'Where are you going, mister?' I asked one of them as he passed me.

'I'm going to war,' he answered. It seemed a dramatic answer, but the street looked just the same as always as I went back indoors for my tea. That night I went out alone to walk on the cliffs. All the fairy lights were out, and the town lay in darkness below me. I looked out across the Channel and wondered where the Germans were – I half expected to see the first ships coming across the water right away. I had no idea what war was going to entail, for me or any of us.

3. Working on the Land

For the first few months after war was declared there was a strange atmosphere in the town. Ramsgate had always been a bustling, cheerful place in the summer months, thronged with holidaymakers who came mostly from London. Now the streets were oddly quiet and dark; the visitors had all left and the lights had been extinguished. Almost overnight, and without any sign of the distant enemy, the town seemed to have died. The only indication of war was that we were all ordered to go to the Westcliff Pavilion to collect our gas masks.

'Why do we need gas masks?' I asked my Guardian, and she said that it was likely that the Germans would start bombing us soon. People of her generation were very fearful that gas would be used, because they could remember its terrible effects on soldiers in the First World War. I had no such memories to worry me. I was afraid of what war might bring, but as a fifteen-year-old I was not taking a close interest in its progress. I saw the headlines on the newspaper stands, but I was more concerned about how it would affect my ordinary everyday life. The first winter of the war was extremely cold, and the start of rationing meant that our meals in the children's home grew even more frugal.

Still the war had made very little impression on me until the summer of 1940, when I saw the boats going out from Ramsgate harbour to the evacuation from Dunkirk. Every kind of boat left, both large and small, until the harbour was virtually deserted.

'They're going to fetch the troops back from France,' my Guardian said, 'because we have lost the war in Europe.' Now we all felt that the enemy was really on the doorstep. Our army had ceased to attack and was being driven back to the Channel beaches, and once the soldiers had been brought home by the little boats in this haphazard and amateur evacuation, all that would be left for them to do was to defend us. However, there was no time to be afraid or despondent about the course of the war, for the immediate practicalities had to be dealt with. From Dover, Deal and Ramsgate the boats had set out, and they would soon be returning with weary and injured troops. The authorities appealed for donations of food and blankets, and my loyal and patriotic Guardian, like everyone else, set about baking dozens of bread rolls. I was sent home from the ironmonger's by my boss, and told to do whatever errands were needed in the town, so I had an exciting time running to and fro between the home and the harbour.

By the time the first boats returned, the sea front was a hive of activity. The WVS was brewing up tea and there were huge trays of mugs and tables full of bread rolls waiting. Soon the harbour was busy once again, as the soldiers and their rescuers came ashore and were wrapped in blankets and given cups of tea. Some army staff had appeared and were taking down names and numbers and trying to establish some kind of organisation, and I watched as exhausted soldiers and civilians alike slumped down wherever there was space to rest.

Much later on I realised that what happened next made an indelible impression on me. I could see that the sea just outside the harbour was still thronged with little boats bobbing on the waves, waiting their turn to come in, but suddenly an order was given and the men stopped coming ashore. In the area of the fish market, at one side of the harbour wall, a space was cleared, and long trestle tables were set up and covered with white cloths. Proper chairs were produced from somewhere, places were laid with cutlery and glasses, and I believe even some military silver appeared on the tables. Then, from two or three boats, some senior officers came ashore, and they sat down at the tables and were served a full lunch. No mugs and blankets for them: they had obviously commandeered the most comfortable boats for their journey, and now they were being entertained in the most incongruously civilised manner. Meanwhile, the rest of us, civilian volunteers and soldiers alike, waited around for half an hour while they ate. Then they left, the tables were cleared, and the disembarkation continued. The other ranks who had been left shivering in their open boats outside the harbour wall were allowed to come ashore. This display of the army's regard for seniority impressed me most by its callous disregard for the welfare of the ordinary fighting men.

Shortly after this excitement, the Battle of Britain began. In Ramsgate we had what might be regarded as a ringside seat, and during those summer days and nights I used to go up onto the flat roof of the house to watch the show, just as we used to go up before the war to watch the Friday night firework displays put on for the benefit of the summer visitors. I am afraid that our attitude was very little different: I watched Spitfires and Hurricanes firing and wheeling and diving in the air as if it was a spectacle put on for our amusement. Even though I had looked with curious eyes at the wounded soldiers with their makeshift bandages limping up the harbour steps only a few weeks before, I still didn't think about the pain inflicted by war. I had no sense that this was a terrible struggle going on between three or four pilots, no thoughts that someone was going to be wounded, or that when a plane nose-dived into the sea or land that someone was dying. I was simply fascinated by the aerial display of light and sound.

Once the Germans began shelling the south coast, our nights were endlessly disrupted by air-raid sirens and explosions, and at last we began to have some realisation of what war meant. We were the first and last port of call for German bombers, so even if they passed over us on their way inland to some more important target, they would frequently offload any remaining bombs on us on their way home. Night after night was spent in the discomfort of the air-raid shelter, and we lived in a state of constant tension. In the spring of 1941, my Guardian told me that she had decided that Ramsgate was too dangerous for children, and she had succeeded in arranging evacuation for almost all of us. I assume that her motive was genuine, although none of us ever thought to ask how she would make a living when there were no children left for her to care for. In fact she had some conversions made to the house and immediately re-opened it as a home for the elderly, so I feel that she may have laid her plans carefully.

I was to go to Bigwood Camp in Berkshire, a privately run camp, to work on the land; this time, at last, I really was leaving the children's home behind for ever. I had mixed feelings as my Guardian saw me on to the train, for my previous attempts at leaving the home had not been entirely successful. However, I wasn't sorry to be leaving Ramsgate: the threat of German shelling had scared me considerably, and I was glad to be going somewhere safer. Miss Butler's final words to me about my real name, 'Clarke – with an e,' were merely mystifying. I could not see what use such a tiny snippet of information was ever likely to be, but it felt like some kind of parting gift, the only thing she was able or willing to give me. I knew that a stage in my life was coming to an end, and I was excited and apprehensive about what awaited me.

I was collected at Radley station, near Oxford, and driven up to Bigwood Camp in a small car. The camp consisted of about thirty wooden huts in Radley Wood, and there were about sixty boys living there. It seemed to me that I had simply moved from one children's home to another, and all the pressures of communal living were just the same. Each hut housed six boys, sleeping in bunk beds, and there were separate huts for toilets, washing, and cooking and eating. However, I was very well treated there, which was an improvement on my past experience. The beds were comfortable and the only housework we were expected to do was to keep our own huts clean. Above all, the woods were all around us, so I could always go off on my own to get away from the other boys.

The food was good, too, after the children's home. We were given breakfast and supper at the camp, and a packed lunch to eat while we were at work; sometimes we would eat our sandwiches during the morning and then tell the farmer we had no lunch, and the more kindly among them would find us something more to eat. Although rationing was in force everywhere, there were plenty of vegetables available in the countryside, and chickens and rabbits too. In many small communities there was also a certain amount of unofficial pig-killing which was never registered, and I saw this several times in Radley. The meat was stored and shared around, so there was often extra ham and bacon which never passed through the rationing system, and the other farm workers would give us some extra food at lunch time.

We were supposed to be a pool of labour for local farmers, much needed when so many men were away fighting, and so each day a bus would collect us from the camp and drive around the countryside, dropping us off at farms around Radley, Abingdon and Oxford, and picking us up again in the evening. The idea was that we would work for a farmer on trial for six to eight weeks, and then if he found us acceptable he would employ us formally; we would then go and live in at the farm, and our place at the camp could be taken by another boy.

I worked for Stephen Dockar-Drysdale at Wick Hall Farm, Radley, and after my six weeks were up I was duly taken on as a farm labourer, and moved into the double-fronted bungalow with the family: the farmer, his wife Barbara (always known as 'Pip'), two children called William and Sarah, and their Nanny. Although they appeared to me to be an ordinary family, they turned out to be very different. Pip had always been interested in child development, and 'by the outbreak of the Second World War she was sufficiently well known as one who "understood" children to become involved with the emergency evacuation programme in Berkshire.' (Obituary by Christopher Beedell in the *Independent*, 8.4.99.)

After the war they moved to Standlake, where they founded the Mulberry Bush School at the invitation of the Home Office, taking with them a mix of evacuees and children who had been referred to them by psychiatrists. The school did pioneering work with difficult and disturbed children, and Pip subsequently trained as a psychotherapist at the Tavistock Clinic and at the Maudsley Hospital. She became very well known and lectured and published on the subject of therapy in child care.

At the time, of course, I knew nothing of her interests. I always got on well with her, although I did not like her husband much. I suppose I was too old to be of clinical interest to them.

Every day I got up at five thirty and went down to the cowshed to help the cowman with the milking – by hand at first, though later on some machinery was installed. I enjoyed milking: the cows were placid creatures, though occasionally a bucket would be kicked over and the cowman would shout at me to take more care. The milk was poured into a cooler and funnelled into churns for bulk deliveries and into bottles for ordinary delivery. While it was being bottled and put in crates I helped the cowman to clean out the milking shed, and at about eight o'clock I went back into the farmhouse for breakfast. Then the farmer and I would get into the farm van and drive to Abingdon to deliver the milk. We got home again at about ten, when I was sent out to work on the land with the other farm workers, hedging or ditching.

This marked the beginning of a wonderful time for me: I loved being out in the open air all day. At haymaking time I would sit on the hay rake, with the horse in front, and go up and down the field turning the hay. When we were harrowing I would do the same, walking up and down all day with the harrow, with the horse in front pulling, and me behind. I thoroughly enjoyed everything I had to do: for once in my life I was on my own; no one was ordering me about, and no one was punishing me. I was given one order for the day, and told what to do, and then I was left to do it without interference. Working on the hay rake, pulling the handle and making the long straight lines of turned hay was immensely satisfying; I was never bored. I used to sit up on the rake, singing at the top of my voice, all the popular songs I knew, feeling deeply happy. I didn't care if the rain poured down or the sun shone: I was free.

At harvest time we left the horses and mechanisation took over, in the form of a tractor and a harvesting machine. The tractor was driven by an old man called Frankie Pitter, whom I grew to respect and like because he was a true countryman, very kind and a good teacher. He taught me a lot about the land, how to recognise plants and trees and the wildlife all around us: when we stopped for our meal breaks he would say, 'Look at that skylark,' or 'Look at that blue-tit,' or 'Those are rabbit tracks.' He taught me to know something about the place I was working and living in, in the most natural way. He was well known in the village as a good man, liked by everyone, and he was gentle and patient. He was probably only in his sixties, but he seemed immensely old to me, and he always had time for me.

While Frankie drove the tractor I sat on the binder behind it, an amazing Heath-Robinson contraption compared to today's efficient combine harvesters. A long blade cut the corn and a conveyor carried it up into a chute where it was tied. At intervals I would pull the handle and the bundle of cut corn would drop out onto the ground, where it was gathered up by one of the other men who were building the stooks in lines across the field. Sometimes I would get down from the machine and take my turn at stooking, collecting four or six bundles and leaning them together so that they supported each other. I enjoyed both these tasks: they were fairly leisurely and clean, and had a rhythm dictated by the speed at which we chose to work.

The threshing machine was a different matter. It was owned by a firm called Thatcher Brothers, and they toured the countryside at harvest time with a huge steam engine and the thresher which was attached to it by a drive belt. My job was to stand on top of the thresher and cut the string on the bundles of corn as they were thrown into the threshing machine. The corn emerged from the back of the thresher and was poured into bags weighing over a hundredweight. These were carried away by the men and I could never understand how they could lift such heavy sacks. Mine sounds like an easy job in comparison to theirs, but it went on for hours and hours, and I used to get terrible blisters on my hand and cuts on my finger from the continual use of the sharp knife I held. However, the alternative job was worse. When I complained, saying, 'Please take me off this job, look at the state of my hand,' the reply was, 'Get round the bloody back there, boy.' At the back was the dust box, where I had to bag the dust and chaff that came out of the threshed corn. This was long before any Health and Safety considerations were dreamed of: there were no masks to cover your mouth, so we breathed in the choking dust, and the tickling, irritating pieces of chaff worked their way into your clothes and against your skin. At the end of the day I was jet black with dirt and dust. It was a job I hated. In addition, we had to work at the speed at which the thresher could digest the bundles of corn, so we had to keep feeding it with corn all day at the same rate: the farmer was paying for its hire, so there was not to be a moment when it stood idle.

The day was a long one at the height of summer: we would stop for breakfast at about nine thirty, and again for lunch, when we would sit down under the shade of a hedge or under the harvester itself, and get out our cans of cold tea to drink; some of the men used to bring beer. Most of us would have the same food: bread and cheese (you could get an extra cheese ration if you were a farm worker) and a big onion. We would sit and talk, and laugh, and joke, and it was a very friendly, happy atmosphere. It may be only the romanticised view of memory, but it seems to me, looking back, that the sky was always blue, the days were long and hot, and I was happier than I had ever been in my young life.

All of this seemed to be the most immense change in my life: in the space of a few months I had gone from the brutality and harshness of the children's home to a new world of freedom and kindliness, where I was treated as an equal by the men I worked with, and respected for doing a good day's work. That experience of working on the land changed me; I was shaped by that environment, and I felt that I knew where I belonged. No matter what the weather, I was nearly always intensely happy.

The house where I was staying was Wick Hall Farm (not Wick Hall, which was large mansion nearby), and when I returned home in the evening I would have my evening meal with the family. My last job in the evening was to wash up after this evening meal, every night except Sundays. Other than these meals, I spent no time with the family; I didn't much like Stephen Drysdale, my employer, though I went out with him to deliver milk. Once, when we were returning home from working on the farm, he said to me,

'Ever drunk beer, my boy?'

'No,' I answered.

'Well, it's bloody well time you did,' he told me, and pulled the van into the Bowyer Arms, his favourite local pub.

'What do you want, bitter or mild?'

I didn't have the faintest idea, never having tasted either, so I said, 'I'll have half a pint of bitter,' and he bought it for me. I thought it was disgusting, but didn't dare say so.

One Sunday evening after our evening meal, Stephen said to me as I was leaving the room,

'David, I've been talking to Pip, and we've decided that you ought to wash up after dinner on Sunday night, as well as the other six evenings in the week.'

My response was quite irrational. 'What, you want me to wash up on Sundays as well, when there are two women in the house?'

I am ashamed now of my reply, which betrays a very dated view of what we thought of then as 'women's work' – though in my defence I can at least say that I had spent most of my life doing housework, so it was not an entirely chauvinistic remark. It was not this, however, which annoyed my employer. He retorted,

'How dare you call my wife a woman? My wife is a lady. You're sacked. I want you to leave this house next Saturday at noon.'

I had no idea what I would do. I worked the week, and on Saturday at breakfast he reminded me again.

'You know you've got to leave here at twelve noon, don't you?'

'Yes, I do,' I replied.

'And you're going to go, aren't you?'

'Yes, I am,' I said. I was too proud to plead for my job or to let him know how desperate I was feeling. I had nowhere to go, so I prepared a bed for myself by taking some hay from the barn and putting it down in a dry ditch on the edge of the farm, so that I would at least have somewhere to sleep. The farm was at one end of a long private road called Thrupp Lane, which led to the main road between Abingdon and

Radley. At twelve o'clock I left the farm and started walking down this lane with my small suitcase: all it contained was a pair of wellingtons and a jumper – the total sum of my worldly goods at the age of seventeen. Just then a car came up: it was another farmer from Blewbury who had been calling at Wick Hall.

'Where are you off to, boy?' he asked.

'I don't know. I've been sacked,' I told him.

'So where are you going to sleep tonight?' he said.

'I've got some hay in the ditch down here,' I replied.

He leaned across and opened the passenger door of the car. 'Jump in,' he said. 'I'll give you a job.' So I drove off with him, having found my next job not five minutes after leaving the previous one!

I spent that first night in a house in the village at Blewbury, but when I started work at seven thirty next morning I asked the farmer if he could find me somewhere else to stay.

'The bed was full of bugs,' I told him. 'Look, I'm bitten all over. I spent most of the night sitting up in the kitchen to get away from them!' He found me a room in the farmhouse and I moved in there.

I was always grateful to him for giving me refuge when I was desperate, and he was a kindly enough employer, but I left him after only a month. I was keen to get back to Radley because I was missing my girlfriend.

Back in the early days at Bigwood we were allowed to use bicycles belonging to the camp, and we would often go into the nearby villages to look for girls. One summer evening I cycled into Radley, and under a beech tree close to the pub I noticed a pretty girl sitting alone on a wooden seat which surrounded the trunk. She was looking very sad and thoughtful, so I went and sat down beside her and we got talking. Her name was Beryl, and she told me that she had just come from her father's funeral. All her family were at the pub – family gatherings were often held there because the cottages were so small – but she was too upset to be with everyone else, so she had slipped away.

The story of her father's death was a sad one. Fred was a foreman for the Great Western Railway; during the First War he had been in the trenches, but railway work was vital war work so he had not joined up this time. He had been working at Abingdon Station, where two women were loading tree trunks onto trucks with the aid of a large crane. They were finding it slow work, as the crane was operated manually by a heavy winch handle, so he had offered to help them. As he was turning the handle, the safety catch broke, and the handle spun round and hit him, lifting him off his feet. He died three days later of his internal injuries.

The sequel to this was yet another example of the injustice meted out to the working man. Fred had been a member of his union, and the union later told us that they had discovered a 'cover-up' by the railway. A GWR representative had come from Swindon to look at the crane, and while examining it had replaced the catch with another – not brand new but well used – so that they could claim that the accident was due to negligence on the part of the operator, not to faulty mechanism. Because of this, his widow Evelyn was entitled only to workmen's compensation, and nothing could be claimed from the employer. She had to go to the County Court at Oxford to claim it, and the judge's words to her broke her heart.

'You are going to be awarded three hundred pounds in compensation,' he told her, 'but you will not receive it all at once, because people like you are liable to squander it all immediately, and then scrounge off the state.' This was to a woman who had worked hard all her life and brought up a family on a tiny wage, practising economies such as that judge never dreamed of. Once again I saw the ignorance of those who wielded the power in our class system.

From then on I met Beryl regularly, and our relationship flourished. When I made the move to Blewbury I missed her so much that I cycled the ten miles to Radley two or three times a week, and in the end I decided to find another job closer to her.

This time I went to work for Arthur Greening, who had farms at Radley and at Sunningwell, and I worked on both, milking the cows at Radley and then cycling to Sunningwell to do field work. Greening was a dreadful man to work for. He was a churchwarden, and told me several times that I ought to go to church, but he was a very poor advertisement for his religion. He was often the worse for drink, and would come roaring and shouting after us as we went out to do our work. He drank even more than usual on Mondays and Wednesdays, when he took cattle to market at Abingdon and Oxford and brought others back on the truck to the farm. Often, in his haste to get the cows unloaded, he would hit them so hard with his stick that the skin on their backs split open.

When I moved back to Radley I lodged at first in a small bungalow in the village, but this was rather a nerve-wracking place to stay, as the owners drank heavily, and were always fighting and threatening each other with knives. I then lived for a while with Beryl's aunt and uncle, Ernest and Doris Villebois, and finally moved into Beryl's home and became the second lodger. I enjoyed living with them; all the proprieties were observed as Beryl slept with her mother in one bedroom, and the lodger and I shared a double bed in the other. The other lodger was not a particularly clean individual, and Beryl's mother Evelyn often mentioned the fact that he didn't like washing. As he was fond of warming his feet on mine during the night I was glad when he got married and left the house for good. As Evelyn said on his wedding day, 'I bet he still hasn't washed his feet!' My girlfriend and her mother thus became my first real family: they both gave me the love and affection I had never experienced before. It was my first real home.

Once again the cycle of the year went round on the farm, and I was happy enough in my daily work and happy to have Beryl to court in the evenings. All this time the war was grinding on, though it had little effect on us out in the Berkshire countryside, apart from the increase in rationing: first clothes, then soap and petrol. The USA had entered the war and every other man you saw seemed to be in uniform. I had joined the Abingdon Home Guard, but this did not feel like a particularly useful contribution. We spent many nights standing on guard on a railway bridge over the River Thames, armed only with broomsticks; what use they would be if the Germans had landed I could not imagine. In addition, I was tired of being shouted at by Mr Greening, and I thought that perhaps it was time I did my bit for the war effort. At the beginning of 1943 I made up my mind: I would volunteer to join the Royal Marines.

4. A Quiet War

I was eighteen and a half when I took the bus into Oxford and went to the army recruiting office in George Street to volunteer. I was given an eye test and a reading test, which I just about managed to pass, and told that I would be notified by letter. In due course the letter arrived, accompanied by a railway warrant: I was to report on 12th February 1943 at the Royal Marines barracks at Eastney, Portsmouth.

I was tremendously excited at starting out on this new venture; I wasn't really thinking about the war much, or about fighting: it was simply something new to do. Beryl and her mother saw me off from the station, and I made my way down to Portsmouth and on to the huge barracks at Eastney, where I was duly processed and handed my kit.

What I had completely forgotten over the last two peaceful years was that the whole of the south coast was essentially a war zone, and that first night was terrifying. Ack-ack guns were blazing, air-raid sirens sounded and we all spent the night in air-raid shelters; bombers flew overhead and the ground shook as the bombs fell. The next morning we were all weary after our sleepless night, but no concessions were made as we started out on our training as Royal Marines.

The Marines prided themselves on being a tough and disciplined outfit, and their training reflected this. Now at last I began to reap one of the few benefits of my upbringing in the children's home: I was already independent, and although I had left behind Beryl and her mother, that experience of family life was too new for me to miss it deeply. I was used to looking after myself, to doing my own washing and cleaning, and I was not accustomed to any kind of family support and affection. Many of the other young men in my barracks had come from loving families where Mother did all their washing and cooked their meals: away from home for the first time, homesick and miserable, they were shocked and horrified to find themselves doing their own washing, cleaning the toilets, or clumsily trying to peel potatoes. One or two of them would cry at night, smothering their tears in their pillows, but I was quite happy. Even my long days of manual work on the farm were paying off: at last I was beginning to fill out and grow stronger, and disciplinary measures like being told to run round the parade ground for an hour didn't worry me.

'What's the bloody matter with you, Buckle?' barked my sergeant. 'Nothing seems to frighten you.'

'Sarge, my Guardian could teach you a thing or two about discipline,' I replied.

It was true; I was used to being punished every time I did something sloppily, so I had learned to do things properly the first time. The kind of spick-and-span neatness the Marines required of the barracks came naturally to me, and I seldom had to do anything twice. This didn't always endear me to my fellows, and I was knocked about a bit once or twice, mostly because I was always so irritatingly cheerful. But on the whole I got on well with the other men, and I took to life in the Royal Marines like a duck to water.

I realise now that during those early weeks the Marines had one objective: to establish control and discipline over a group of young men and teach them to work as a team. This meant, to a certain extent, stripping away their individuality. Everything had to be done by the book, in the right way, at the right time. We woke when the bugle sounded, washed when we were told to, responded to orders with instant obedience. Other eighteen-year-olds resented the loss of their freedom and autonomy, but I was already an old hand, and felt quite at home.

I also had a good time in my off-duty hours, going into Portsmouth to the pubs and clubs and cafes, drinking and dancing and flirting with the WRNS. After two years in the sleepy Berkshire countryside, I was having a taste of the bright city lights – or what would have been bright if there hadn't been a blackout. I was having the time of my life.

After fourteen weeks of square-bashing we were getting impatient to do something.

'When are we going to war?' we asked, but the reply was always, 'When you're trained well enough to do the Marines proud.'

The Marines were so jealous of their reputation as an elite fighting force that any men who joined during the war were labelled as HOs – Hostilities Only. We were recruited under wartime requirements and not considered suitable as long-serving soldiers, and so promotions seldom came our way. However, my enthusiasm and efficiency meant that I was quickly promoted first to Lance Corporal and later to Corporal, and I was delighted to be a success at something at last.

We were to serve in Combined Operations, mainly to be in charge of landing craft, so we were sent to North Wales for six weeks' training in signalling, navigation and gunnery, with two weeks being devoted to each. I remember once sitting in a theatre in the Marines camp in Towyn with a crowd of enlisted men, being lectured by an officer on how to aim shells at moving aircraft. The officer was one of the old (public) school, with an accent so posh I could have done with an interpreter.

'Just imagine,' he said in a high-pitched voice, 'that you are in the garden and a cat is running like stink acrawse the lawn. To hit it, you would aim a stone just in front of it. Any questions?'

'Yes – what's a bloody lawn?' asked a cockney voice from the audience, to shouts of laughter and applause.

After this we went up to Invergordon where we did some very serious training in handling the boats, with ships lying offshore and firing live ammunition at the beach. Then we were all taken on board ship, together with our landing craft, and sailed all around the west coast of Scotland, across the Irish Sea (which was a very rough passage) and back round to the south coast. There we waited in Portsmouth Harbour for D Day.

Our little flotilla of boats was deputed to carry messages and sailing orders to the fleet of huge battleships lying in the Solent. After a few weeks of this I knew Portsmouth Harbour like the back of my hand, and could navigate my way anywhere by compass, even in the thickest fogs: our two intensive weeks in Wales were paying off. It was during this time that my Company Sergeant-Major came and told me that I had to report to the Brigadier at Brigade Headquarters. I was duly marched into his office and stood to attention in front of his desk.

'Corporal Buckle,' he said, 'you are to be promoted to the rank of Sergeant, and I have to tell you that you are now the youngest Sergeant in the Royal Marines. Congratulations.'

'Thank you, sir,' I replied. 'Does that carry a higher rate of pay?'

'Get him out of here before I change my mind!' roared the Brigadier, and I was ushered out. It was not the most effective piece of wage-bargaining I was to attempt.

In the end I never went to France for D Day. We delivered all the orders to the battleships, and the next day the harbour was deserted except for a fleet of large merchant ships still lying at anchor. They had been fitted out with derricks to take our landing craft, about twenty-four on each side. We went on board and sailed out into the channel, but stopped about half way across. In accounts of the war which concentrate on the D-Day landings, this back-up fleet is never mentioned; many of us believed that we were the emergency service. If the landings had failed, we would have been called upon to effect an evacuation from the beaches of Normandy: presumably the War Office wished to avoid another Dunkirk.

After this we returned to Portsmouth and were sent for further training to a camp at Windrush, on the Oxfordshire–Gloucestershire border: back to peaceful Middle England. I was having a fairly uneventful war so far: lots of training but no fighting action, for which I was thankful. In any case, I had other things to occupy my mind, because I had finally decided to get married.

Back in the spring I had been posted to Brightlingsea for some boat-handling training, and I spent a lot of time walking on the cliffs. One Sunday I went up to Westcliff and spent hours walking up and down, turning things over in my mind. Beryl had become more and more important to me, and the trivial nature of my light-hearted flirtations at Portsmouth had perhaps shown me by contrast how deep my feelings for her had become. I was a poor candidate for marriage: I had no experience at all of normal family life, no model on which to base any idea of how a husband or a father should behave. I also had no sexual experience, because I had always been absolutely sure that I didn't ever intend to father a child outside marriage.

It is hard in these more liberal days to explain how deeply the stigma of illegitimacy had affected me. At a time when almost all children were brought up in the traditional nuclear family, fathers were absent only because of death or war service. Illegitimacy was deeply shameful; unmarried girls who became pregnant would have to leave home to spare their families the disgrace. There are even records of unfortunate girls being placed in mental hospitals, because they were 'morally incapable'. I have no idea what happened to my own mother. To have no known parentage and to be brought up in a children's home was deeply embarrassing; I tried hard to avoid telling people anything about my background, and if forced I would say that I was an orphan. At an age when young men seldom relate their sexual activities closely with procreation, I was acutely aware of the consequences of casual sex, and it had held me back from intimacy with any girl.

If I marry, I thought, it will have to be for life; nothing will be allowed to break that bond. Any children of mine will be brought up in a home as loving and secure as I can make it, and if I don't know how, then I will simply have to learn how to make a marriage work.

On my next leave I proposed to Beryl, and we were married on 30th December 1944 at Radley Church. All Beryl's family and friends clubbed together with their ration books to provide food for about a hundred people including, to my great delight, my old friend Grace from the children's home. At last I had a family of my own.

Now the war was drawing to a close and the Allied Forces were advancing across Europe. At Windrush our training was for the 'Special Brigade' which was designed for one task only. We were to go to Germany and capture the SS headquarters at Lubeck, then to Kiel Harbour to capture the German U-boat pens and naval ships, and on to Flensberg to capture the German naval High Command. We spent a great deal of time sitting in huts studying maps and aerial photographs of Lubeck and Kiel, learning the lie of the land.

When at last we moved out we travelled from Tilbury to Ostend and into Belgium where we were billeted in an old Belgian cavalry camp. The accommodation was not exactly luxurious: we had to make palliasses out of straw from the stables to sleep on. The next day we went on to Brussels airport, from where we were to fly to Luneburg Heath. As I was a Sergeant I was in charge of my own squad, and I got the men lined up by the runway, waiting for our transport. The Dakotas were bringing in ex-prisoners of war from Germany and ferrying us back by return. One man called out to me as we waited.

'Sarge, I can't go in one of them things. I've never been in a plane before.'

'Neither have I,' I replied, 'but we've all got to.'

'I can't,' he said. 'I'm too scared. I've shit meself.'

We had to get him cleaned up before it was our turn to climb into the plane.

'Hey, where are the parachutes?' asked another man. An officer was checking us all in and he answered with a grin. 'If anything happens, jump out and you can pick one up on the ground.'

At Luneburg Heath we were loaded onto lorries to go to Lubeck. On the way we passed through the outskirts of Hamburg, and nothing could have prepared me for the shock. For the first time in my life I saw the true effects of war: Hamburg seemed to consist only of vast piles of rubble, storeys high, and out of the rubble came Germans waving white flags made of handkerchiefs or sheets. I didn't see any dead people, but there were dead horses and dogs and cats everywhere – the result of recent bombing by the allies.

At Lubeck we reached our objective: the SS headquarters for the whole of the Schleswig-Holstein area, but once again our experience of war was something of an anti-climax. When we tried to enter the building the SS officers inside pulled down huge steel shutters which blocked every doorway; we tried on all sides of the building but it was effectively sealed. We thought that at last we would see some active service and fight our way in, but an officer told us to withdraw. We waited around at a safe distance, and after a while we heard a huge explosion: the Marines had blown up the building with everyone inside it. When we returned it was just another huge pile of rubble like the others we had seen.

Back on the lorries once more, we drove on through the night to Kiel, arriving at about five thirty in the morning. We were cold and tired, but there was nowhere to sleep. We waited on the pavement while the officers went into a nearby block of flats, and soon sleepy Germans were coming out of the doors. They were mostly old people and children, and they were lined up and marched away – I have no idea where. Then we were told to go in and occupy the flats, so we got into the warm beds the inhabitants had just been thrown out of. It was just another example of what victorious armies do, and I was a part of it. When we woke up later we casually looted the flats, taking whatever food or belongings we fancied. Again, at this distance from the war it seems callous behaviour, but it was a wartime situation, and we were full of the propaganda that had made us hate the Germans, so we thought it was our right.

The children's home at Tooting. I am third from right, one of the oldest children.

Sitting behind the table with my friend Mohan. Grace is sitting on the extreme left.

At Crouch House, probably about 1933.

Miss Butler, as she was usually dressed each day at home.

Miss Butler doing voluntary service during the war.

Top: Bigwood Camp, Radley, in 1941. Sir Ralph Glynn, MP for Abingdon, addressing what he hoped would be future Tory voters. I am standing alone on the left, wearing what I am proud to see is a distinctly sceptical expression!

In uniform, aged nineteen.

Our wedding day, 1944.

The Iberia.

*Our first wedding
anniversary, 1945.*

*A trip to Ramsgate in 1950
with both our sons, to visit
Miss Butler.*

Above: Election results, Bournemouth East, 1955.

Below: Election results, Banbury and North Oxford, 1959.

Above: A banner found in the Plough Inn, Witney, known to have been last used on Witney Green in 1913. (By courtesy of the Oxford Mail.*)*

Below: Addressing a student rally against racial discrimination in St Giles, Oxford, in 1968. (By courtesy of the Oxford Mail.*)*

1969: Discussions at Pressed Steel Fisher, Cowley, with Jack Jones, General Secretary of the TGWU, and Mr Edwards, the plant director. (By courtesy of the Oxford Mail.*)*

1982: Standing on the bridge over the Cowley site. (By courtesy of Financial Times Pictures.*)*

Later that day we went down to Kiel Harbour to capture the U-boat pens there. We were amazed by the U-boat bunkers, which were made of concrete up to twenty feet thick. On top we could see the tiny indentations made by the bombs dropped by the RAF: mere pinpricks which had had no effect at all. Inside there were large numbers of miniature, two-man submarines, being built on a sort of production line. We captured these and went on to the German warships lying at anchor in the harbour. My job was to go to the captain of each ship, and receive from him the ship's papers and flag, together with his personal papers and his revolver.

There was no fighting involved in these transactions: the war was coming to an end and agreements had been made about the hand-over of the German war machinery. Our Special Brigade, too, had seen no action, so we were perhaps a little more detached than some of those we were working alongside: naval officers and men who had spent the war being torpedoed and shelled in mid-ocean, or soldiers who had fought their way painfully across Europe. They had a much more immediate hatred of the Germans we were now capturing. I went with a naval officer down onto the mess deck of one ship, where we found a number of German sailors, all very drunk, passing around a bottle of schnapps. We had sent them all up onto the deck, when another sailor came into the cabin carrying a tray of eggs. The officer with me shouted an order at him in German, telling him to drop the eggs and come on deck. He began to argue – presumably because there was nowhere to put the eggs down – so the officer drew his revolver and simply shot him in the leg.

One of the ships in the harbour was the *Iberia*, which before the war had been a passenger ship. On investigation it proved to be in use now as a brothel ship for naval officers. Our Brigade took the officers prisoner, and for some reason made all the women jump overboard; they were later picked up in boats and taken ashore.

Meanwhile, on shore, German soldiers were arriving from Norway and Denmark. They were organised into groups and ordered to give up their ammunition and guns, which were thrown into a huge pile. Most hated of all were the SS officers, who had been responsible for some of the worst wartime atrocities; they had all taken the precaution of removing the SS insignia from their uniform collars, but sometimes the mark was visible, where the fabric was less faded – a tell-tale sign. Others were betrayed by their own men: an officer would approach the arms pile and the men would shout 'SS' to alert us; they seemed to be as much hated by the ordinary German soldiers as by their enemies.

These officers were subjected to horrifyingly brutal treatment by our own army. Several times I saw them loaded with sacks filled with the scrap iron and chains which were lying around on the dockside, and forced to run up and down the railway line along the harbour wall. There was no special purpose in this other than an attempt at humiliation. I also saw one German propped up against a wall while a British soldier emptied a Bren gun magazine of tracer bullets at him. When I and some others complained to the army officers about this, they shrugged it off.

'What do you expect? We're in a war zone,' they replied. I am ashamed to have been associated with this kind of cruelty, but I did nothing more to try to prevent it. We, after all, had been training in the quiet English countryside for the previous months, while some of these army officers had been liberating Belsen. The sights they had seen there were almost indescribable; they didn't want to talk about it much, but they wanted to vent their anger on someone, and the SS was a very handy target.

We left Kiel after ten weeks, having completed most of the tasks we had set out to do, taking prisoner German naval and army personnel and securing weapons, ships and submarines. Ours was not so much an active war as a tidying-up and supervising operation at the end; I was grateful, as I had no taste for the cruelty I saw even in this relatively peaceful period of the war. We returned to England with the first of the merchant ships taken under the Potsdam War Reparations Agreement. The ship was not the only reparation being taken: most of the soldiers had looted small items at some time during their stay in Germany, but the Commander had a Mercedes loaded at the front of the ship and a sailing boat at the back!

We set off down the Kiel Canal and into the North Sea. We treated this like a rather leisurely cruise: we had few duties and plenty of time on our hands; the war was over, and we were on our way home. One officer, however, thought that we could make better use of this time, so he called all the COs together. He pointed out to us that all of our Special Brigade were HOs, so we would be leaving the Marines after the war, and we should be preparing ourselves for civilian life. Some of the older COs gave talks about 'Life at Work', pointing out that the post-war world was likely to be different from whatever we had known before. One Sergeant-Major in particular had vivid memories of the worst years of the Depression, and he was convinced that the time had come for radical changes in the roles of workers and managers. In the old days, he said, the employers had all the power: they could hire and fire at will, and the working man had to take whatever treatment was meted out to him.

'Don't let the bastards do to you what they did to us in the twenties and thirties,' he said. 'Organise yourselves into unions and get your rights through organisations.'

These were new ideas to me, and they gave me much food for thought during that voyage. The power of the employer was certainly something I had experienced, and perhaps it was even more deeply entrenched in the countryside, where ownership of land was everything; you took it for granted that the landowner or the farmer had all the power. But I didn't intend to go back to that life: there was no future in it for me, and I didn't want to be a labourer all my life, especially as I now had a wife to support. But I could see that whatever work I ended up in, the same power structure would be operating, unless there was some mechanism by which it could be changed. I thought back over my experiences of work so far. With no skills and very little education, I was always going to be at the bottom of the pile, being told what to do by someone else. Only in the Marines had I begun to shine, and had achieved promotion, because there was a well-established career structure which took account of hard work and willingness. But then I thought back to the Dunkirk evacuation, and the serving men left shivering in their boats while the officers were welcomed ashore, and the cup of tea and a bun offered to the soldiers compared to the hot lunch served to the officers. Even in the services the system was rigged to favour the people with power. I decided that I was not going to be a victim of the system any more. The Marines had taught me to take some pride in myself and my achievements, and I was not going to be pushed around.

My first opportunity to assert myself came almost immediately when we returned to Portsmouth to be demobbed. Last time I had been in Eastney barracks I was a private – now I was a Sergeant, and entitled to eat in the Sergeants' Mess. Although it was run on a self-service basis, it was a much grander affair than I was used to, with silver cutlery laid out on the tablecloths. I had just collected my meal and sat down, when a Colour-Sergeant tapped me on the shoulder.

'Move,' he said.

'I don't see why I should,' I replied, looking round the half-empty Mess. 'There's plenty of room here.'

'Move, Sergeant,' he said, and when I refused again, he fetched the RSM, who was President of the Mess.

'Sergeant Buckle, move yourself,' he ordered.

'Why should I?' I asked.

'Don't argue,' he replied. 'That's the Colour-Sergeant's chair you're sitting in.'

Determined to the last, I stood up and turned the chair upside down. 'I can't see a name on it anywhere,' I said.

The Colour-Sergeant intervened again. 'It's been my chair for the last fifteen years,' he said.

'What?' I asked. 'While we've been fighting a bloody war, you've been sitting on that chair?'

I moved in the end – I had no wish to be put on a charge a few days before being demobbed – but I still felt that what the Marines saw as insubordination I saw as rebellion against unreasonable authority.

Our demobilisation came early; the Royal Marines didn't want the HOs on their force, so now that the war was over they got rid of us as fast as possible. I travelled home and was met at Radley Station by Beryl and her mother. I was a civilian again, with a new life ahead of me. We walked back through the summer evening to Eve's thatched cottage, and I remember thinking to myself, 'I'm home. And I'm never going to leave this village again.'

5. Work and Learning

I did not realise it at the time, but the end of the war had brought me to an important landmark in my life. The only things my childhood had given me were bad memories, a nervous disposition, a poor education and a bad stammer. Now I was an adult, and my time in the services had at least improved my self-confidence and taught me that it was possible for me to succeed. I was married, and the love of my wife had made an immense difference to me. I had never known the support of a family before, but now it gave me the confidence to face new challenges and set out on a new way of life, and a reason to do so. I wanted a better life for my wife and children.

Few of the conveniences of the modern world had come to Radley in 1945. We lived with Beryl's mother in her thatched cottage: two low-ceilinged rooms upstairs and two down. With so little space you would hardly think any room could be kept 'for best', but the front door opened straight into such a room: it held a piano, a three-piece suite and a sideboard, and a table covered with a velvet cloth on which stood an elderly but apparently immortal aspidistra. We seldom used that front parlour. There was a latched door in the far wall which led through into the kitchen, a larger room where we mostly lived. In it there were two rexine-covered armchairs and a chaise longue to match, two scrubbed tables, a dresser which held all the china and food, and a three-burner paraffin stove with a tin oven, on which we did all the cooking. Paraffin was sold from a van which visited the village once a week.

Upstairs were two bedrooms, one leading directly into the other, and each with a small-paned window set into the thatch. They were difficult to furnish because of the sloping walls and uneven floors, but each held a double bed and washstand, a small wardrobe and a chest of drawers. After our two sons were born we had to find space for two cots as well.

Our water came from a well in the garden, a simple stone-lined hole without even the traditional winding mechanism: instead we used a bucket on a long pole. Whenever the bucket fell off the hook it was difficult to re-attach because the well was so deep and dark, with ferns growing down the sides. It was not uncommon to find a frog or black leeches in the bucket when we hauled it up; village wisdom said that this showed that the water was good to drink. In dry summers our well dried up and we had to use a deeper one in a garden across the road.

With all that effort to get water we learned not to waste it. The garden shed contained a copper for boiling water, and a zinc bath hung outside, used once a week. Another shed held two bucket toilets – one for us and one for the next-door neighbours – separated by a flimsy wooden partition. We disposed of the waste by digging a deep hole in the garden and burying it – one of my regular tasks. This is the secret of the magnificent vegetables grown in village gardens at this time!

This was the world I had come home to, where village life had changed little for hundreds of years, and people worked hard in fairly primitive conditions.

A few days after my return I met Arthur Greening, my old employer.

'I hear you're demobbed, David,' he said. 'Do you want to come back and work for me?'

'No, thank you,' I replied. 'My days of slavery are over.' I felt this to be true. Although I had happy memories of my days of working on the land, I knew that a lifetime of manual labour wasn't what I wanted, and I had also taken to heart the words of the Sergeant-Major on the ship coming home. I didn't want to be at the mercy of a farmer's whim; I wanted a proper job with proper rights of employment.

In any case, the Royal Marines had already fixed me up with a job. I was to work at the Royal Naval Air Station at Culham as a storeman and forklift truck driver. Spare parts for aircraft were delivered to Culham and I had to sort them and send them to the appropriate hangar. No skill was required, and I was paid £4 10s for a forty-four-hour week.

Beryl's uncle was also working there as a lorry driver, and he was a shop steward for the Transport and General Workers' Union. He asked me to join the union and to be a shop steward for the other workers on the site. This was just the sort of thing I had had in mind, and it seemed to be a real opportunity to work to safeguard the interests of the working men, so I agreed.

One of the interesting aspects of working at Culham was the fact that the people in charge of the operation were all senior naval officers, but the work force was composed of civilians, most of whom had been in the armed forces during the war. We were used to treating these officers with respect, but we were fully aware that now we were all civilians, and no longer under the same jurisdiction as before. The officers, however, were not used to dealing with civilians: they would bark out orders and expect instant obedience.

Our first clash came over the matter of pay: not the amount, but the method of delivery. The officers expected us to form up to receive our wages just like a pay parade in the army. The system was that we had to line up in front of a long table. An officer would shout, 'Buckle. Four pounds, ten shillings and sixpence.' Seated at the table would be three ratings, one with a pile of notes in front of him, one with a pile of silver, and one with the coppers. We would pass each in turn and the pounds, shillings and pence would be put into our hand.

This was what we objected to: we were no longer servicemen, so why should we have to put up with services treatment? This was long before the days of payment by cheque, but in civilian jobs, people normally received an envelope with the cash inside – they certainly didn't have the amount of their income shouted aloud in front of everyone else. As shop steward, I approached an officer and explained our objections, and asked for our pay to be prepared in packets. He refused. The next Friday we refused to line up in military fashion.

'What's wrong with the men?' asked the officer in charge. 'Why aren't they lined up?'

'We want to be treated as civilians,' I replied. 'We want our pay in packets.'

'No, you can't have that,' he said.

I stepped forward, tipped up the table, and sent all the money rolling on to the floor.

'If you wouldn't mind,' I said, with great politeness, 'put our wages into packets, and we'll pick them up on Monday.'

On the Monday morning our pay was waiting for us in packets – three days late, but we all thought it was worth it.

After that our relations were always good. It seemed to me in that first encounter that it wasn't just a case of the workers challenging the management, but rather that the management had first challenged the workers: they were treating us in an unsuitable fashion, and our action was responsive rather than provocative. This was an important principle in union activity, I thought. So often the status quo is taken for granted, and any action by the workforce is seen as a 'demand', suggesting that once one is granted, the demands will be insatiable. I saw it differently. Too often we assume that because things have always been done in a certain way, that way must be just, or suitable, or at least adequate. Instead it is frequently the case that unfair burdens have been placed upon workers for a long time, and in that sense the management exploit them or make unfair demands on them. It is in response to such unfairness that workers finally act.

I left Culham in 1950. By then my two sons had been born – Alan in 1947 and Peter in 1949 – and as we were overcrowded in the cottage, we applied for and were given one of the new council houses in Radley, where we have lived ever since. We asked Eve whether she wanted to stay in the cottage or come with us, and she chose to come with us. We promised her that our new home would be her home too, and that she would never be turned out. She lived with us until her death in 1978.

I could not afford to pay the rent and feed my family on my Culham wage of £5 7s 6d, including overtime, so I applied for a job at the Pressed Steel Works in Cowley, part of the extensive works serving the car industry in Oxford. I was offered a job on the production line as a spot welder, earning £15 a week on a piece-work system, a huge increase in wages. I was shown how to do the job by a foreman who showed me round: I didn't like the idea of factory work, but I needed the money, so I accepted it.

On the Monday morning I reported for work and got into trouble at once. I was told to go to work on the punching jig – a quite different job from spot welding. I complained that this was not the job I had been offered and accepted, and when this got little response I asked to see the shop steward. The foreman called him over with a few prophetic words:

'We're going to have problems with this one!'

Once again I had to back down in the end, and on the advice of the shop steward I took the job on the punching jig. I didn't think much of that, but I knew that I had no alternative.

The factory was a nightmare, like a black hole. The technology was primitive, the machinery filthy and noisy. There is no creativity or individuality in a factory: essentially you are another part of the machinery, pulling a lever or performing tasks which so far no machine has been invented to do. At that time, Health and Safety at work was a new concept, one which had had little effect on the car industry, and there were many accidents.

We worked on piece work, which meant that we were paid according to the amount we produced. It meant putting in the maximum effort in the minimum time, and we worked in a gang of about eighty men in one area, sharing the earnings from our particular phase of production. This in turn meant that we put pressure on one another – the younger men drove out the older men who perhaps couldn't keep up the pace. It was very divisive. Men would often tell the foreman, 'Get that bastard out of the gang, he can't keep up.' If the individual was not replaced, but we could somehow manage to take on his share of the work, then that meant extra money for all of us, as we took on his share of our joint earnings. On the other hand, piece work meant that we learned how to control our own work schedules. We could find out how many pieces we needed to produce, and then pace ourselves to get it done. This understanding of work effort and production rates later became useful when we wanted more participation in the management of the plant.

The environment was unbelievably unpleasant and dangerous, with arc welding and gas welding going on, and smoke and lead dust everywhere. Most of the machinery was unprotected, and no one wore face masks, eye shields or breathing masks. In the discing booth men worked at smoothing and polishing car bodies, where molten lead had been loaded onto the spot welds on the back seams of the bodywork. When the sun shone down through the glass panels in the factory roof, it picked out the lead dust as it hung glittering in the air. At tea-breaks we would eat our sandwiches with hands black with dust and oil; if we spat our saliva was black.

There were no extractor fans, so when it got too hot, men would go up onto the roof and take the panes of glass off to provide ventilation. This was fine unless there was a sudden summer storm, when the rain came in and we were treated to an impromptu firework display, as all the electrical circuits sparked and shorted, and we had to go home because the power went off. For someone like me, who had felt such keen enjoyment in farm work and being out in the open air all day, it was a living hell.

One of the worst aspects of factory work for me was its repetitive nature. As you worked on the production line each identical item would arrive, be subjected to a process lasting between one and two minutes, then it would pass on and the next one would arrive. I once worked for three and a half years on a job with a ten-second time cycle: lift the piece of metal, hit it, turn it, hit it again, throw it in a box; lift the next piece, hit it, turn it, hit it again, throw it in the box; lift the next piece ... How many ten-second cycles are there in a day? A week? In three and a half years? That was the sum total of my achievement in those years: that number of items processed.

It was often too noisy to talk, or the next man was too far away, so you learned to occupy yourself with your own thoughts, or else to become an automaton. Much later on I was involved in building the side of a car with another man. I remember going back to work after our morning tea break, and starting off, each moving round doing our allotted tasks. I had begun to get involved in politics by then, and I was thinking about a speech I was going to make at a meeting that night, and going over the words in my head. A moment later I heard my mate say, 'Right, David, time for dinner.' Three and a half hours had gone by without my being aware of them, nor, indeed, of having any conscious recollection of the physical activity I had been engaged in.

One of my best friends at Cowley was an ex-coal-miner, Bill Lowe, who had left his Cheshire home some time in the 1930s to come looking for work in the expanding car industry. He had been a member of the Communist Party for many years, but resigned his membership when the Russian army marched into Hungary in 1956. He studied *The Economist* every week, and spent much of his spare time reading and making notes for the evening class in economics he attended. For nearly fourteen years a small group of us held a daily debate during our lunch break in the works canteen, discussing every political subject under the sun. In the early 1950s, during one of these lunchtime discussions, Bill suggested the idea of a Park and Ride scheme, to reduce traffic in city centres. He was often well ahead of his time! Bill taught me as much as anyone about the real problems of working in a factory, and understanding, to some extent, the capitalist system which held the workers captive.

During the 1950s the car industry was used by the government as an economic regulator through the tax on the hire purchase payments usually necessary for the purchase of a car. This could affect the industry badly, and jobs were never secure. Sometimes there would be plenty of overtime available, and for three or four months we could put in an extra two hours every evening, five days a week, and work all day on Saturday. Then the tax would rise, the market would collapse, and no new cars were needed: the entire workforce would be shut out for a fortnight without pay, or else there would be extensive redundancies. In one year there were 35,000 redundancies from the company in the Midlands area alone.

The shop stewards tried to circumvent this pattern by introducing the system of worker participation. We would insist on being given advance notice of the number of cars we had to produce – and the number of cars being produced across the road in the Morris plant which our Cowley works were also feeding. This would enable us to pace the work steadily, so that we made the right number of parts and avoided the swings between pressurised work rates and layoffs. We decided that although the market was being affected by government policy, our conditions were also being affected by poor management which allowed over-production at one time and forced redundancies at others. It was clear that our system worked better, and eventually we managed to achieve more control over our work rates; however, the system of worker participation was never formally recognised as a scheme within the factory.

I was involved in my first strike quite early on. At the Pressed Steel plant where I worked, all the unions were recognised; across the road at the Morris plant, unions were not allowed (owing, I suspect, to Lord Nuffield's influence). A man named Frank Horsman was elected as the senior shop steward for the Transport and General Workers Union at Morris, and the union sought recognition. The management refused to recognise either Frank's role as shop steward or the existence of the union for the purposes of negotiation. This triggered an official strike at Morris, where the TGWU members were desperate to have some official voice with the management. They sent a message to the union at the Pressed Steel plant to come out on strike too: if we stopped producing the car bodies, the whole Morris operation would grind to a halt. I was the shop steward for eighty members who came out on a two-week strike.

We were striking for a principle: that workers should have the right to be represented in talks with their employers – fundamental democracy. If the union was not recognised, then the workers had no voice, no chance to state their case or request changes in their conditions, because the management could simply refuse to speak to them. To request formal representation was scarcely a revolutionary move in a supposedly democratic society.

Our objective was only partly achieved: at the end of the two weeks an agreement was made at national level by Frank Cousins, General Secretary of the TGWU, that the union should be recognised for bargaining purposes in the Morris plant, but not Frank Horsfield as senior steward. He was offered a job at the neighbouring Pressed Steel car plant, not a part of BMC at that time. The offer of a job but with a different employer caused resentment within the TGWU in both plants. We all felt that Frank Cousins should have supported the original claim, and we were angry that he had in effect done a deal behind the backs of the local people. In spite of claiming that he believed in the power of the union, at the crucial moment he had abandoned these principles. In Pressed Steel we were beginning to earn our reputation for supporting union activists.

I worked at the Pressed Steel factory for fourteen years, from 1950 to 1964, and for nine of them I was a shop steward. Factory life in itself didn't teach me much, other than how to detach myself from my noisy, dirty surroundings, but being a trade unionist quickly taught me one thing: if you wanted to be effective you needed to be able to talk to people. And if you wanted to talk to people properly you needed to be articulate, to express yourself properly. You had to know what you wanted to say: to have ideas, think clearly and understand the principles of what you were trying to achieve. In other words, you needed an education. It was something I had missed out on.

I was a pretty poor hand at all of these things. I couldn't speak well: I still had a bad stammer, which got worse when I was nervous. I had never been much good at reading, because I had missed so much schooling, so I didn't have much vocabulary at my disposal. Not reading meant that I wasn't exposed to much in the way of abstract thinking: in the factory you dealt with objects, not ideas; it was a very practical place. So I was a hopeless case, really. The only thing I did have was determination. I cared passionately about changing things for the better. I had always been at the bottom of the heap, disadvantaged from the start, and I had soon realised that no one was about to give me a hand up. Anything I wanted to achieve I was going to have to do for myself. I wasn't afraid of anyone, though; in spite of my stammer and my poor education I was ready to stand up for my rights and the rights of others. But I needed better equipment to do it with.

The first thing I did was to enrol in a correspondence course for Basic English. I read the advertisement in the newspaper and thought that it would improve my vocabulary, so I sent off a postal order and eagerly awaited the arrival of the first lessons. It was a disaster. My reading was still slow and laborious, and I simply couldn't make head or tail of the material they sent me. It was like trying to read a foreign language. I realised that whatever I was going to learn, I needed someone to teach me in person, someone who could explain things to me. That was when I saw the poster for the Workers' Education Association.

The W.E.A. was founded in 1903 to give working people like me a chance to add to the limited education they might have received at school. Among the courses advertised was one on British Constitution and another on Economics, and those were what I enrolled for. The evening classes were held at Rewley House, in Oxford, and after work, tired after a ten-hour shift, I went along and started my education at last. Here I didn't feel at a disadvantage, because all the other students were working men like myself. The teacher was Maurice Shock, and he loved his work: he took us seriously, helped and encouraged us, and taught us to think for ourselves. No question was deemed stupid: we were never made to feel small.

Each week we were supposed to write an essay, and at first I made excuses to try to get out of it. I had no idea where to start; my handwriting was awful; I had no ideas. Maurice was helpful but implacable: I was going to have to try. At first I wrote only a paragraph or two, but with his encouragement I gradually found that the words began to come more easily as I wrestled with the new ideas he was giving me. It was the same with speaking: I found it impossible at first to speak in class, because of my stammer and my hesitancy: I didn't think I had anything to say, but then something would fire me and I would struggle to express myself.

Maurice knew us well, and he knew the backgrounds we came from. He believed that it was our assumptions about ourselves that held us back more than anything else. One evening in class he asked,

'Anyone here ever been to the theatre? No? There are tickets here if you want them.' He had bought tickets for *Titus Andronicus* at Stratford-on-Avon.

None of us had ever been to the theatre, and we had scarcely heard of Shakespeare. All that was intellectual stuff – you didn't get taught that at Elementary School. We all went, and it amazed us. The next week Maurice asked what we thought of it, and my hand went up straight away.

'I was mystified,' I said. 'I keep reading in the papers about all the horrors on films and television, how they encourage violence, and how we need censorship to protect people from such programmes. Yet the middle classes have been watching this stuff for ages and no one seems concerned about them!' It was the longest speech I had ever made in class, and I hardly stammered at all.

Once again my self-confidence was improving. I'm not sure whether I was determined, or just arrogant, but I felt that I could make a difference to things if I tried. I had joined the Labour Party in 1951, because I believed that it was the only party which supported and understood the working man; in the same year I was co-opted onto the Radley Parish Council to fill a vacancy between elections. That was when I started involving myself in the affairs of Radley Village, as feudal a tiny society as you were likely to find in that post-war period.

The village school was a case in point: the rich people sent their children away to boarding school, but the ordinary village children had to put up with a dilapidated building with a leaking roof and bucket toilets. Just up the road was Radley College, an exclusive public school set in many acres of grounds and with the best facilities anywhere in the country: the contrast was striking. In my role as a governor of the village school I wrote a report on its condition: the overcrowded classrooms with dangerous coke stoves to heat them, the lack of sanitation and the single cold tap, the stinking duck pond, the absence of playing space.

When I delivered my report I took it to the home of the Chairman of the Parish Council, Mr Hellard, a master at Radley College.

'Look here, Buckle,' he began patronisingly, 'I don't disagree with what you're doing –'

'Just a moment, Hellard,' I interrupted. He was furious.

'How dare you!' he spluttered. 'You will address me as *Mr* Hellard!'

Uncertainly I replied, 'Then you will address me as Mr Buckle, and we can be equal.'

It was typical of the situation in the village: the class structure seemed immutable. I might not be able to change that (though I certainly would draw attention to it) but I could perhaps do something about the conditions for the village children. The report was sent to the Berkshire County Council who authorised a proper Ministry of Education inspection, and eventually improvements were made.

These experiences, together with my new studies in history and economics, made me even more interested in politics. It seemed to me that it was only through politics that any change could come about, change which from the point of view of the working man was long overdue. In 1952 I went as the Abingdon constituency delegate to the Labour Party Conference in Morecambe. It was a time of change within the Labour Party, too, as it established its identity more firmly and moved generally further towards its left wing. I was in the hotel bar one evening when Herbert Morrison and Hugh Dalton came in from the National Executive Committee meeting. They both looked thoroughly shaken, which was not surprising: they had both just been voted off the National Executive. Morrison had been a lifelong member and also a senior minister in the previous Labour government, but his time was over: now he was regarded as too right-wing for the new image. The Bevanites were taking control of the Executive and the whole party was about to become more radical.

It was an exciting time to be involved in politics, even at the local level. I was on the General Management Committee of the North Berkshire Labour Party at the time of the by-election in Abingdon in 1953, and took part in the selection of Ted Castle (Barbara Castle's husband) as candidate. Nye Bevan and Hugh Dalton came to Abingdon to help with the campaign, but for all their support for the working man,

I felt that they did not wholly understand the countryside mentality. I took Hugh Dalton to a farm worker's cottage to canvass, because I knew that the man was a Conservative. Hugh was astonished – he simply couldn't believe that a farm worker could vote Tory. Of course, the constituency being what it was, Ted stood very little chance: Airey Neave, the Conservative candidate, was duly elected.

The following year, 1954, I was a delegate at the Labour Party Annual Conference, and gained an insight into the difficulties of other manual workers. On the first morning I went down to breakfast and sat at a small table with one other person. We got talking and I discovered that he was a delegate for the National Union of Mineworkers.

'What's it like, working down a mine?' I asked him.

'Look under table, lad,' came the reply.

I didn't understand him and repeated my question, and got the same answer. Then I bent over and looked into the tiny dark space under the table, sheltered by the long tablecloth on both sides.

'That's the space I have to crawl in for three-quarters of a mile at the beginning of each shift,' he said, 'before I can even start work.' It was a vivid lesson in the dangers and difficulties faced by the miners.

It was at the same conference that the Labour Party debated German rearmament. At the end of the debate, when the vote was taken, I was in my delegate's seat at the back of the hall. It was a card vote, and as the tellers worked their way down the hall it was clear that Arthur Deakin was not in his seat at the front. Arthur was the TGWU General Secretary, and his card vote was worth 800,000 – capable of swinging the end result. The cry went up, 'Where's Arthur?', and just then the rear doors swung open and Arthur, a portly man, hurried down the hall. He reached his seat just before the tellers did, and then couldn't find his card. He was hunting frantically in his pockets to shouts of 'Where is it, Arthur?' from the assembly. Then just as the teller reached his row he stopped scrabbling around and his hand shot up with his card in it – there were resounding cheers and the vote to support rearmament was saved.

I loved all this excitement: I was developing a taste for politics and it seemed, rather like the armed services, to be an arena where hard work, enthusiasm and persistence might pay off. Consequently I offered to stand in the 1955 election. I knew, however, that as an untried candidate I was unlikely to be offered a good constituency. The Labour Party held two lists: winnable seats and marginal and unwinnable seats;

I was only going to be offered one of the latter, but nevertheless I was interested to have the experience of fighting an election. I was one of four candidates invited to the Labour Party selection conference at Bournemouth East and Christchurch, and I was selected twenty-one days before polling day.

I enjoyed the campaigning. The Conservative candidate was Nigel Nicholson (the son of Harold Nicholson, the historian), and he was a very left-wing Conservative, standing against capital and corporal punishment. I was campaigning on a moderate platform of opposing gun-boat diplomacy and supporting the United Nations: so close were we in stance that the Bournemouth Echo published both our photographs, asking their readers whether they could identify which was the Conservative and which the Labour candidate.

On another occasion I met the editor of another local paper together with a prominent local Conservative (not Nigel). We were interviewed together, and disagreed strongly throughout. At the end of the session I reached across to shake hands with the Conservative, and was astonished when, instead, the man spat in my face.

'Well, there's a story for you,' I said to the editor, as I wiped my face and the Conservative stalked angrily away.

'Not in this constituency,' replied the editor, and indeed his story did not mention the incident.

Naturally, I lost the election, but I lost something else too: I went to Bournemouth with a stammer and I left without it. Somewhere in the heat of debate, trying to make a swift retort to hecklers, I became unselfconscious enough to let the words flow freely. I would advise any stammerer seeking a cure to fight a General Election!

All this time I had continued with my W.E.A. evening classes: I still had plenty to learn, and I knew I had benefited immeasurably from Maurice Shock's kindly but firm teaching. In all the time I knew him I never detected what his own politics were: he was totally objective and academic, and the only thing he would not tolerate was sloppy thinking. He was Rector of Lincoln College from 1987 to 1994, and is now Sir Maurice Shock; he is a man to whom I owe a great deal.

There were two other people I met at this time who also had a profound influence on me: Ilsa and Arturo Burea. I first met Ilsa when we were both on the General Management Committee of the North

Berkshire Labour Party, and she invited me to her home at Buscot, where I met her husband Arturo.

Arturo was born in Madrid, and was immensely proud of his humble origins. During the Civil War he became famous all over Spain and Latin America for his anonymous broadcasts as the '*Voz de Madrid*'. A well-known author and an expert on the poet Lorca, he was also head of the Foreign Press and Censorship Bureau of the Republican Government. After the Civil War he fled to Britain where he took up British citizenship; from 1940 onwards he broadcast weekly talks to Latin America for the BBC, under the name of Juan de Castilla. Ilsa was his second wife; Viennese by birth, she had studied political sciences at Vienna University, and had been a leader of her generation in the stormy nineteen twenties and thirties. She emigrated for political reasons, first to Czechoslovakia and then to Spain, where she joined the Republican Party and met and married Arturo. During the Civil War they met Lord Faringdon, who had gone to Spain to fight with the Republican forces and was working as an ambulance driver. When the war was over and it became clear that they would have to leave Spain, he offered them a lodge on his estate at Buscot Park.

These people were educated, cultured, and cosmopolitan; I was uneducated, uncultured, untravelled; getting to know them was a shock and a stimulus. They opened my eyes to new ideas and experiences; they introduced me to music, art and literature. I was spellbound. I developed a close relationship with them both, and they became like a second family to me; if Beryl's mother Eve had become like the mother I never knew, then Arturo was like a father. I loved them both dearly.

I often spent weekends with them, talking and listening, learning about the politics of Europe between the wars. They were both very astute: to have lived in Austria during the rise of Fascism and in Spain during the Civil War meant that they had first-hand experience of some of the formative political movements of the century. It was in their warm living room, talking late into the night over a bottle of wine, that I received my real political education.

Even going into their home was like entering a different world. Ilsa often had the radio playing, but it was always what is now called Radio Three – they were the only people I knew who listened to classical music by choice. Even the food was different. At home, every main meal consisted of the standard British meat and two veg. Here I learned to eat paella, pasta and even calamari, with the dye used to make a black sauce. The first time I saw it I said, 'You'll never get me to eat that.' Then one Friday evening when I arrived, Arturo blindfolded me and said that he had a surprise. He led me into the kitchen where he gave me a taste of something on a spoon.

'What is it?' I asked. 'It's beautiful!' Then he removed the blindfold and showed me.

'Well, I had to find some way of breaking down your British conservative eating habits,' he said.

In exchange, I would tell them about my experiences of growing up in England between the wars, and about life in the car factory. Arturo used some of these stories in his regular broadcasts: 'You are very well known in parts of South America,' he told me.

They had beautiful books full of reproductions of works of art, many of which they had seen themselves in the galleries of Europe. When I complained about my work in the factory, so dull and repetitive and uncreative, Ilsa reproved me.

'Perhaps your working day is like that,' she said, 'but Oxford is full of museums, galleries, and concerts. Why not try some of them?'

So I started exploring the culture that had been all around me all along, going to concerts and visiting the museums, teaching myself something about history and art. Sometimes we argued: Arturo would get very angry about hunting, which he saw as a cruel hobby of the English upper classes; I would tease him and ask him innocently about bullfighting, a sport to which, as a proud Spaniard, he was irrationally devoted.

It was their influence which encouraged me to start travelling abroad: when package tours began to be available in the early 1960s, Beryl and I saved up and began to take our holidays in places we had never expected to visit. In Italy and France, instead of lying on the beach, we would visit museums and art galleries, bent on earnest self-improvement.

Many years later, after Arturo's death, I visited Ilsa in Vienna. On that trip I was giving some lectures to the Council of Labour (an organisation rather like our TUC) on the subject of the British trade union movement, but I had a good deal of time left for sightseeing. One afternoon I visited a gallery in the Ringstrasse where I discovered a number of wonderful Breughel paintings. It was very quiet there, and I selected a picture which I liked very much and sat down to look at it. After a while a group of people came in with a guide, who was addressing them in both German and English, so I had a chance to pick up some extra information. He led them to a painting at the other end of the gallery, which he described as 'the finest Breughel here'.

'Typical,' I thought. 'In my ignorance, I'm admiring the wrong one as usual.'

When that group left, I moved along to look at it. As I stood there, another guide came in with his group. He took them to stand in front of a third painting. 'This,' he said, 'is the finest Breughel in the gallery.' After that, I decided that I would learn to trust my own taste.

In 1959 I was selected as candidate for Banbury and North Oxford – another Tory stronghold and so another Labour 'B' list seat, but at least I had the benefit of being fairly local. This election had an interesting sideline for me in that the Party asked if I would agree to be sponsored by the TGWU. Under this scheme the union would pay a modest sum (between £100 and £500) into the constituency funds, and also pay for an agent and fund the campaign. This seemed perfectly reasonable to me, and it never occurred to me that the union might want any further return for their investment other than knowing that they had helped to install a Labour MP.

There were two stages in the process of sponsorship: first I was interviewed by the regional committee of the TGWU (including Jack Jones) who recommended me to the second stage, the General Executive of the TGWU. There I was interviewed by the General Secretary, Frank Cousins, and the Finance and General Purposes Committee.

At that second interview I was asked many of the same questions as at the first one, and then at the end Frank Cousins took over and fired much bigger questions at me.

'What do you think about the Cyprus crisis? You have eight minutes for your answer.'

'Describe the economic situation of this country. You have ten minutes.'

It was gruelling and exacting, and I thanked my stars that I had worked so hard in those British Constitution evening classes with

Maurice. I was ready with my answers and tried to show understanding of both politics and economics. Then at the end came a final question which astonished me. Frank Cousins said,

'I want you to assume that you have become a Transport and General Workers sponsored MP and you are now in the House of Commons. Will you give me' (and he did not say, 'the TGWU') 'a solemn undertaking that you will not ask any questions or make any speech in the House on any matters relating to the TGWU or industrial relations without consulting me?'

So much for my studies of politics and British Constitution. If I had learned anything from them, it was that a Member of Parliament is a representative, not a delegate.

'No,' I replied, 'I won't. I'm prepared to give an undertaking not to ask any question or give any speech on TGWU matters in Parliament before consulting you. But beyond that I'll regard myself as the representative of the constituency that elects me, not as a delegate of the union. I'm ashamed that the General Secretary has put such a question to me.'

'Then that terminates this interview,' said Frank Cousins.

'I've no doubt about that,' I answered, and walked out. I knew that I had made an enemy.

I was not given TGWU sponsorship, but I was still the selected Labour candidate, even though some on the committee, such as John Ennals, thought that I was too moderate and right-wing for the Labour Party. I worked hard at my canvassing and campaigning (I lost a stone in weight, running round the constituency and attending meetings), but I did not win. Nevertheless, the result was respectable: the Conservative had only a 6,000 majority over me, and I felt that I had acquitted myself well. As we left the County Hall at Oxford where the count had been held, Beryl and I crossed the car park to get to the bus stop and make our way home. We passed the successful Conservative candidate, Neil Marten, sitting on the wall with his wife and son, drinking champagne.

'Get back to that fucking factory where you belong,' he shouted after me.

It made me proud to be a Labour supporter.

6. A Role in Society

The WEA classes I had been attending had broadened my outlook on life; I was developing not just an awareness of the society in which I was living, but also a social conscience. My political activities were one expression of that: I wanted to make changes in the way society was run, so that it was not just for the benefit of those at the top of the class structure.

I had discovered that a whole range of seminars and meetings were available in Oxford for anyone to attend, on a variety of subjects, including some on crime and punishment. Some of these were run by the Probation Service, and I went along and listened and occasionally contributed. It was at one of these meetings I met Dr Mary Watson, a Labour County Councillor and a magistrate on the Abingdon bench. She knew me through our Labour Party contacts, and at the end of the conference she made a suggestion that astounded me.

'Have you ever thought about being a magistrate, David?' she asked.

The word 'magistrate' rang bells for me. Long before, when I was in the children's home, my Guardian used the magistrates as one of her stock of threats.

'If you go on being naughty,' she would say to us, 'I'll take you before the magistrates!' She never explained exactly what would happen to us then, so we assumed that it would be something terrible. I could hardly believe that someone was now asking me if I wanted to be one of them.

I was very hesitant. Didn't you have to be 'someone' to be a magistrate? Didn't you have to be well educated? Common sense told me that my instinct was wrong, but I couldn't help feeling that surely you had to be rich. Or posh. Or something. Not a factory worker who grew up in a children's home. That wasn't the sort of person who was a magistrate.

Mary patiently explained that I was wrong on all counts. Magistrates were ordinary local people who administered justice in local courts: it is a very long time indeed since the magistrate was the local squire or landed gentry. There are no academic qualifications: magistrates have to be intelligent and show common sense, the ability to think clearly, look at issues objectively and come to reasoned decisions. Nothing more. You didn't need a law degree: legal advice was available from the Justices' Clerk. She thought I was the sort of person they were looking for. I was far from convinced, but agreed that I would think about it.

The next thing that happened was that I received an imposing-looking letter from the Lord Chancellor's office, asking whether, if I were appointed, I would accept. After a great deal of thought, I wrote back and said that I would. (I may say that things nowadays are done very differently: candidates are interviewed thoroughly in a two-stage procedure designed to find out not only a great deal about personal circumstances and attitudes, but also about aptitude and ability to reason and understand evidence.)

In January 1961 I was invited to go to Reading Assizes to be sworn in, because at that time Abingdon was still part of Berkshire. It was the first time I had ever set foot in a court of law, and I was deeply impressed by the proceedings. There were fifteen of us, and we were sworn in by Judge Claude DeVine, a very colourful character who came from a famous legal family. We had to take the oath of allegiance to the Queen:

> I swear by Almighty God that I will be faithful and bear true allegiance to Her Majesty, Queen Elizabeth the Second, her heirs and successors according to law.

This is the same oath that is taken by all members of the judiciary and by members of Parliament. Then we took the judicial oath:

> I swear by Almighty God that I will well and truly serve our Sovereign Lady, Queen Elizabeth the Second, in the office of Justice of the Peace, and I will do right to all manner of people after the laws and usages of this realm without fear or favour, affection or ill will.

It was the last few phrases which impressed me the most. That was my burning wish: to see that right was done to all people no matter what their class or background, their contacts or lack of them. 'Without fear or favour, affection or ill will' convinced me that this really was something I could do wholeheartedly.

After we had been sworn, the judge announced that he would like us all to stay behind in the court.

'We have a very serious case coming on, and it will be useful for you all to listen to the evidence.' So we all stayed behind and listened to the case: it was a charge of burglary, and the defendant was pleading not guilty. After the case had been heard, the jury retired to consider their verdict and the judge turned to us.

'Now,' he said, 'I want each of you to spend five minutes summing up the evidence we have just heard, and giving me your views on it and whether or not you think the defendant is guilty. The jury are the ones who will decide, but I should like to hear what you say.'

This came as a tremendous shock, since most of us had never been in a court before and had no understanding of the procedure. I was shaking with nerves – I hadn't expected this! – but we all did our bit, and I think my contribution was pretty poor. Then the jury came back and found the defendant guilty. We heard the pleas of mitigation, and then retired again while the judge considered his verdict. Once again he turned to us and asked us what we considered would be a suitable penalty.

It was a serious burglary (of a dwelling-house at night) and the defendant had a long history of similar convictions. The consensus among us novices (who had never yet sat in a magistrates' court) worked out at an average of about five years' imprisonment.

'You're a bunch of softies!' exclaimed the judge. 'Five years? Seven years at the minimum. Follow me!' and he marched us all back into court and announced the sentence.

That was my first experience of the legal system, and I began to wonder what I had let myself in for.

Even before I got to court I began to run into trouble with friends and colleagues at work, and other members of the trade union movement. Several of them thought I was getting above myself, and that I had sold out to the bosses.

'You're part of the establishment now,' they told me. 'You're operating a system designed to oppress working people. What are you doing, getting involved with this kind of thing? Who are you to pass judgement on other people, who are suffering under a class system that you have suffered under?' Those were the kinds of comments people made to me, and they did concern me. However, I had developed a different view. As far as I could tell from the courses I attended, the vast majority of the people appearing in court before magistrates and judges were working class – but the majority of judges and magistrates who were judging them certainly were not.

Surely I could have a minor role to play, in trying to operate a system of justice which had regard for that fact. It seemed to me that many people end up in court not so much through their own fault but because of the system in which they live: their economic, political and social environment can often drive them into crime as a means of trying to survive. That does not mean that we condone criminal behaviour, but that we can sometimes understand some of its causes.

That in itself is important: society finds itself spending large amounts of money on dealing with the effects of crime, and perhaps it would be better to spend some on investigating the causes of crime and on preventing it. A recent National Audit Office survey noted the close correlation between areas of high crime and those of social deprivation and poverty – that surely tells us something. The high crime areas are not mysteriously populated by extraordinary groups of people with criminal tendencies, but simply by people who are sometimes desperate enough to be driven to foolish and criminal measures. I have certainly seen many more inadequate individuals than evil ones in court.

When I was first appointed as a magistrate, the personnel director of the Pressed Steel plant, where I was working, called me into his office. He, too, was a magistrate, on the Oxford bench.

'David, I want to congratulate you on becoming a magistrate,' he said. 'It's a great tribute to the company that you have been selected.'

'Oh, yes?' I said. 'Why isn't it a tribute to the Transport and General Workers' Union, or to me as an individual working-class person? And by the way, unlike you, I'm going to lose money by being a magistrate. Under the piece-work system, I don't get paid when I'm out of the plant. What am I going to get paid by the company for the time I'm out?'

He was horrified by the suggestion. 'If you've accepted the honour of being a magistrate and doing your public duty, you have to accept the costs too. You won't get compensated for loss of earnings.'

However, I got the union behind me and we eventually negotiated the princely sum of 7s 6d an hour for loss of wages – and that went to all the other people performing public service and losing money: magistrates, local government officials and councillors, too. So I managed to do some good for all the others as well.

On the day I arrived for my first sitting I was very apprehensive. At that time the only preparation I had received, apart from the experience in Reading, was nine small pamphlets about 'Being a Magistrate', sent by the Lord Chancellor's Office, and which were no help whatsoever. Nowadays, again, things have changed considerably, and magistrates are given lengthy initial training and regular refresher training to ensure that they are well equipped for their work. In 1961 there was nothing. It astonished me that I could be allowed to adjudicate in a court as one of three magistrates, with no experience at all.

The Abingdon Magistrates Court wasin a lovely old building attached to the Guildhall; parts of it date from the fifteenth century. The court itself was small, with wooden panelling on its stone walls. Along one wall was a shelf holding a row of Victorian leather fire-buckets; above the magistrates' bench hung a large coat of arms. It epitomised local justice: all the formality and dignity of the legal system in an intimate and familiar setting. Outside, across the street, the local market day was in full swing.

At that time almost all the magistrates were local businessmen and professional people; I was the first working-class magistrate – and certainly the first factory worker – on that rural bench. My fellow justices were very kind to me, very polite, and perhaps occasionally a little patronising: I still could not always express myself very well, and I did not have the confidence that comes either with education or with social standing. But none of them treated me with any hostility, and I was very grateful for that.

Magistrates try criminal cases as judges in a public court, as well as taking on various administrative responsibilities such as the control of the sale of alcohol, granting police warrants and taking oaths and declarations. I found all these aspects immensely interesting, but the criminal court is perhaps the most demanding. The magistrates' court is the first stage in the criminal justice system: 97% of all cases begin and end there, and the remaining 3% are the more serious cases which begin in the magistrates' court and are then transferred to the Crown Court to be heard by a judge and jury. Because the offences they deal with are 'less serious', magistrates have limited sentencing powers (currently up to £5,000 fine and a total of twelve months' custody, as well as a range of community sentences).

Sitting in court requires a complex mixture of qualities. Magistrates must approach every case with an open mind, avoiding personal prejudices and resisting coming to premature conclusions until the whole case has been heard. They must be fair and impartial, being attentive and courteous to all defendants and witnesses whether they are aggressive, tedious, confused, timid or antisocial. Magistrates must accept the advice of their court clerk on legal matters, but must then make their decisions independently, unswayed by public opinion or personal or media pressure.

The great strength of the lay magistracy is that it consists of part-time, amateur justices. Judges deal with complex and serious cases and so need extensive legal knowledge and training. Inevitably they are sometimes accused of being out of touch with ordinary people: they are members of the legal profession and as such share a common language and background in their university education and legal training; they may well have achieved their ambitions in arriving at a prestigious and well-paid post. Magistrates on the other hand come from all walks of life with no common outlook other than their willingness to serve the community: there is little prestige attached to the role since they are discouraged from advertising their appointment, and no remuneration since the work is voluntary and unpaid. Intelligence, common sense, integrity and the capacity to act fairly and impartially are more important than formal qualifications. With the aid of the legal knowledge of their court clerk they administer justice in their own community: local justice for local people by local people.

I had a sharp reminder of my theories of justice very early in my career as a magistrate. I was sitting with two other magistrates, both very experienced, one of whom was a very forthright, disciplinarian character, who was chairing the court. We had a case of a farm worker who had been stopped for driving without due care and attention, and he had pleaded not guilty. We listened to all the evidence – he had been driving a tractor along the road from one part of the farm to another – and eventually found him guilty.

'Right,' said my colleague, 'he must be disqualified from driving for three months.'

My years of working as a farm labourer had taught me something about the standard conditions of such work, and I felt that I had to intervene.

'Just a minute,' I said hesitantly. 'Do we know what the full implications of a driving ban might be for this man?'

'We don't need to worry about that, Mr Buckle,' replied the chairman. 'That is a matter for him.'

'Well, I am worried about it,' I persisted, 'and I'd like to check up on the possible consequences. We might be giving him a very severe punishment indeed.'

'Well, all right,' sighed the chairman. 'We'll return to court and say that we are considering disqualification, and get his reaction.'

We duly went back into court, and the defendant stood up as the chairman addressed him.

'What would be the effect if you were disqualified for three months?' he asked.

A voice replied from the back of the court room, where the public were allowed to sit.

'The bugger'll get the sack!'

The chairman looked up at the interruption and said, 'And who are you?'

'I'm his boss,' said the farmer, 'and I don't want anyone who can't drive on the public highway. He'll get the sack.'

I leaned over and whispered to the chairman, 'Can you find out if he lives in a tied cottage?'

The question was put, and the farmer said yes. At this point the defendant spoke up for himself.

'I live in his house, and I've got five kids. If I get the sack we'll all be put out on the street.'

We withdrew into the retiring room again and the chairman, to his credit, said, 'I see what you mean, Mr Buckle. We can't disqualify this man. We will consider a fine.'

I felt that my experience of the everyday living conditions for farm labourers came in useful that day, and I began to have more confidence that I could be of some use as a magistrate. It was a classic example of the fact that the magistracy needs to contain people from all walks of life, and that every one of them needs to make an effort to know something about and understand the problems faced by other people.

Later on I had the experience of dealing with someone from the other end of the economic spectrum. A man had been convicted of a speeding offence, and because of the number of penalty points on his driving licence, the magistrates had the option of disqualifying him for up to six months. He came into court in a very smart suit, and was followed by a barrister carrying a large pile of papers, all tied up with red ribbon and looking very official.

The defendant acknowledged his guilt, but said that there were mitigating circumstances which he wished to be put before us by his barrister, to show why he should not be disqualified from driving. The barrister rose and announced that he intended to call as a witness the chairman of the defendant's company, the '600 Group' – a large international engineering company.

The chairman went into the witness box and gave evidence that the defendant was the company secretary, important not only to the company, but to the economy of the country as well. So vast was the business done by this group, and so vital the man's role in it, he told us, that six months' disqualification from driving would have dire effects on both. As a full-time trade union official, I was very interested to hear all this. When it came to the time when the magistrates could ask questions, I asked him,

'In the event of this man being disqualified for the full period of six months, would you consider supplying him with a chauffeur?'

His response was, 'Certainly not! The only person who has a chauffeur is me, the chairman of the company!' I was tempted to reply, 'What? Even if it affects the economy of the country?' but I kept quiet and merely noted his reply.

At the end of the evidence the barrister rose to sum up, and delivered what he thought was an impassioned plea on behalf of his client.

'Your worships, in front of you stands someone who works hard for his company and his country – not someone who is constantly holding the country up to ransom, like these trade unionists and shop stewards.'

The clerk of the court turned round and gave me a knowing look, and all the local solicitors, who knew me very well, were smothering their smiles. The barrister seemed to feel that he had everyone's full attention, and proceeded to enlarge on his theme of striking working-class shirkers as opposed to hard-working professionals like his client.

When we retired to consider the case I asked the clerk, who advises magistrates on legal and procedural matters, to come into the retiring room with us.

'Do you think I should continue to sit on this case?' I asked him. 'After all the barrister has said about trade unionists I'm not sure I am a suitable justice.'

The clerk, however, was quite firm. 'Of course you are suitable,' he said. 'The barrister's remarks are quite irrelevant: the man has pleaded guilty and you are merely considering the period of disqualification. I'm sure you can put ill-judged remarks aside and be objective.' He turned back with one hand on the door. 'By the way, you may be interested to know that the local solicitors are running a book on how long you disqualify him for!'

In the event we disqualified him for only four months.

This case was interesting to me because of the assumption made by the barrister that he was in a court room among a peer group – members of the legal profession and magistrates who were bound to be middle-class professionals who would share his social standpoint and political opinions. He was wrong on both counts: firstly because I was there, an unexpected (and in those days unusual) element on the bench. And secondly, he did the whole bench an injustice by assuming a stereotype: that the magistrates would all share a common viewpoint. Even in those days there was a healthy range of opinions on the bench, and nowadays this is actively encouraged by the Lord Chancellor's requirement that all benches should reflect a balance in gender, occupation and politics.

I experienced a similar prejudice in the Crown Court. Magistrates are regularly invited to sit alongside a Crown Court judge, and on this occasion I and a lady magistrate from another bench were waiting in the judge's room before court began. The judge arrived and the other magistrate was introduced and shook hands. When I told the judge my name, however, he asked me what I did for a living.

'I'm a local trade union official,' I replied.

Instead of shaking my hand he jabbed me in the shoulder with his finger, saying, 'The trouble with you people is that you do great harm to the economy with all these demarcation disputes, arguing about who does what in the factories. It's time it was stopped, Mr Buckle.' With that he swept into court. I was powerless to discuss the matter with him, though I felt that he didn't understand what the trade union movement was trying to achieve.

The first case was called and we began the business of the day, with all the barristers lined up in front of us waiting for their cases to come on. We had not proceeded very far when a man in a dark blue suit stood up at the back of the court and said, 'Your Honour, may I address you?'

'No, you may not,' replied the judge, without looking up. 'Whoever is interrupting these proceedings, please sit down and be quiet.'

After a short while the same thing happened again; the man stood up and asked to be heard, and was told to be quiet by the judge. I was intrigued by this little performance.

The third time he stood up, the judge threatened that he would be evicted from the court, but asked him what he wanted.

'I am a local solicitor, representing the local Law Society, and we are seeking the right for solicitors to address judges in the Crown Court.'

This was during the early 1970s, and the beginning of the battle between barristers, who could work in all courts, and solicitors, who were then confined to the lower courts. The barristers were shaking their heads in disapproval, and the judge began to talk to the solicitor, emphasising that he did not have the legal right to speak in the Crown Court. While this was going on I wrote a note to the judge. It said, 'You are now involved in a demarcation dispute. Would you like my assistance?'

He turned to me and scowled, the man sat down, and business continued.

When we went out for lunch the judge said lightly, 'Touché, Mr Buckle,' but I was not prepared to let it go at that.

'No, Judge, I'm sorry, but you can't get off that lightly. You admonished me for being a party to demarcation disputes. The legal profession is just as efficient at demarcation disputes as we are in the factories. It's not a working-class preoccupation: the barristers have established the first closed shop in the country.' I felt it was an opportunity to spell out to at least one judge the error of this commonly held idea that the working classes were engaged in dispute for its own sake.

I never found it easy to stand up to those in authority, because I was always very aware, in spite of my principles, that in our society we are not all equal. I was always afraid of being ridiculed for my lack of education. Nevertheless there was another matter of principle on which I was prepared to stand firm.

In 1988 I received a letter from the Lord Chancellor, inviting me to become a member of the Vale of the White Horse Advisory Panel, the group which interviews and selects new magistrates. I was very pleased to be asked, because the selection of magistrates is crucial in the business of achieving the right social and political mix for each bench. However, the letter contained one very worrying statement. It said that if I accepted this responsibility, I should understand that I must keep secret the fact that I was a member of the panel, and that I must not divulge any of the business of the panel to anyone.

I replied to the Lord Chancellor's office, saying that I was honoured to be offered the job, and that I would certainly accept that all the business of the panel was highly confidential. But I could not agree to keep secret the fact that I was a member of the panel. I said that I had never been a member of any secret society in my life, and I did not intend to start now. If that condition could be removed, then I would be glad to accept appointment to the panel; if it could not, then I must refuse.

I waited six weeks for the reply, and when it arrived I was astonished by its contents. It said that I would be the first magistrate ever to join an advisory panel without the condition of secrecy. Subsequently it became general practice that magistrates could be members of their advisory panels without that condition, but I don't claim the credit for the change. I suspect that it was part of a general move towards more openness in many areas of government and legislation. Nevertheless I was pleased that I had not had to give up this opportunity by standing up for what I thought was right – as an individual against the system, refusing to accept its terms.

In the years since I was first appointed the magistracy has seen many changes. Nowadays there is extensive and continuing training, so that magistrates are much better informed about both law and procedure, and they operate common systems of structured approaches to sentencing. In fact, I sometimes think that the pendulum has swung too far. I would never deny the necessity of training, but nowadays a great deal is required of magistrates, both in the number of sittings they must complete each year and the number of training sessions they must attend. I would resist the suggestion that the magistracy should become professional or be handed over to the stipendiaries (paid professional magistrates who sit alone rather than in threes), but I think there is a very real and growing case to be made for a future Home Secretary or Royal Commission to consider some kind of recompense to be paid to magistrates for the time they give up. There is every reason to feel that the government is effectively exploiting the goodwill and sense of public duty of some 30,000 individuals.

Once I was appointed to the local advisory panel I made it my aim to try to redress the balance and find more ethnic minority and working class people to join the bench. Naturally I would never make race or class a priority over ability, but they were aspects of bench 'balance' which I felt had been neglected in the past. There were other problems, though: at a time when industry was 'downsizing' and paring its labour force to the bare minimum, employers were becoming reluctant to release people to perform their court duties, and workers were reluctant to offer themselves when appointment to the magistracy could affect their jobs, their promotion prospects, their income and thus even their pension rights.

In 1988 I attended a meeting with the then Lord Chancellor at the County Hall, Oxford, to discuss the problems facing appointments panels, and I pointed out these difficulties. Subsequently Lord Mackay wrote to 250 major companies in the UK, asking employers to consider the employment rights of magistrates, and urging them to encourage their staff to offer themselves. Nowadays I understand that a certain amount of self-interest is urged upon employers: staff who work as magistrates are given training in the analysis of evidence, structured decision-making, public speaking and negotiating skills, all valuable in the workplace and available as a free bonus for employers!

Most people find that their workplace experience and their judicial experience are mutually beneficial; this was certainly so in my case. Being a magistrate did increase my self-confidence to a certain extent when I had to deal with official bodies, and the skills of listening and analysis which I had learned around the negotiating table helped me both in court and in the retiring room. However, I always felt that it was my personal experience of people which helped me to be a good magistrate. Working as a shop steward did not just involve dealing with employment issues. There were eighty men in my gang at Pressed Steel, and they would bring all their family and personal problems to the shop steward: they would ask for a quiet talk and pour out difficulties with rent, cars, wives and children. Sometimes they needed advice about finances, or letters written to insurance companies (I never let on that this was as hard for me as it was for them), or just a listening ear. It afforded great insight into other people's lives.

One difficulty I had when I first began to sit as chairman was in making pronouncements in court. Sometimes these can be quite complicated, especially where there is a string of offences to be sentenced, or where the bench feels that some explanation will help the defendant understand the reasons for a particular disposal. In those cases my colleagues would often suggest that while we were still in the retiring room I should write down what I intended to say. I hated this, because I had a great fear that they would see that I found it hard to write: my spelling was still dreadful and words did not come easily. I would get round it by listing the main points as I intended to cover them, and saying that I would rather talk directly to the defendant in non-legal language – it was easier for both of us. Generally they accepted this. However, the sensation of trying to hide my inability to write properly made me more sensitive to the problems faced by defendants. Often we would ask a defendant if he had seen certain papers, statements or reports, and if he had not, they would be handed to him in court. If I noted the tell-tale body language of someone who could not read – eyes skimming too fast down the page or the idle flicking of pages until a suitable time had elapsed – I would step in. Generally I found the best solution was to ask if he would like any help in understanding the legal things in the papers, and if he said yes, I would ask the probation officer to go outside with him and explain. The probation staff were always quick to take up the implication and would readily go out and help by reading or summarising the report in private.

Another aspect of being a magistrate is visiting prisons – important since sentencing may include sending people into custody. It always seemed to me that if society was going to spend enormous amounts on keeping people in prison, it should get something for its money: some kind of education and rehabilitation programme designed to make at least some effort towards ensuring that the prisoner was enabled to change his way of life and avoid returning to crime and further imprisonment. Even today, wherever good and imaginative education programmes are in place, the story one hears on visits is always the same: 'We had facilities but the cuts mean that we can't use them,' or 'We can't afford the staff to do this any more.'

At least the modern prisons are better equipped physically than the old ones, even if the regime is still one of punishment rather than rehabilitation. I have never forgotten the experience of visiting Oxford Prison when it was still in use: Victorian buildings, tiny barred windows, slopping-out (this was before the reforms instituted by Judge Tumim and the provision of washing and toilet facilities) and stone walls, dark and depressing.

Some years later, the Oxfordshire County Council had the opportunity to buy the prison back from the government. Under the 1877 Prison Act the control of prisons had passed from local to central control under the Secretary of State. The transfer of Oxford Prison had been agreed with the proviso that should the site and buildings no longer be required for use as a prison by the government, then the County Council would be offered first refusal at the time of decommissioning and sale. The price, fixed at the time, was £9,009, and that was the sum the Council paid to bring the site back under our control. I was an enthusiastic supporter of the scheme, not least because I thought it would be a good thing if no one was ever again forced to spend a period of custody in such dreadful surroundings.

In July 1997 I had the great pleasure, as Chair of the County Council, of receiving the keys of Oxford Prison from the Governor of nearby Bullingdon Prison. Though I had long since retired as a magistrate, I felt that something, at least, had been achieved and that part of my role in society had come full circle.

7. Turbulent Times

In 1963 I had been a shop steward for nine years; that was when Jack Thomas, the highly regarded Oxford District Secretary of the TGWU, told me that he would be retiring the following year and that he hoped that I would succeed him. I was forty that year, and I did not want to spend the rest of my working life as a manual labourer in a car factory. I had given up any aspirations to a career in politics: I had failed to win two General Elections and I did not think I would be offered another chance. After a great deal of thought I decided to apply for the job as a full-time union official.

I was one of ten candidates to be interviewed by Jack Jones (then the TGWU Region 5 Secretary) and Harry Urwin (Assistant Regional Secretary), and I was told that they would recommend my appointment to the General Secretary, Frank Cousins. My one fear was that Frank would remember my last interview with him, when we disagreed about union sponsorship of parliamentary candidates. I need not have worried: in December I received a letter appointing me as Oxford District Secretary Designate, at a salary of £20 per week. I later discovered that not only had I halved my pay, I had also doubled my hours, to an average of seventy per week. I had a hard time justifying that to Beryl.

The plan was that I should work alongside Jack Thomas until his retirement in August, and then take over as District Secretary. I needed those seven months: as the most senior official of the TGWU in the area I was responsible for members who were both manual and white-collar workers in the car industry, government industry, Witney blankets, cement industry, food manufacture, commercial transport, public transport and local government. Learning how all these different companies operated, together with the agreements and negotiating procedures they used, offered me a very steep learning curve indeed.

However, two things made this job the ideal one for me, in spite of the drop in income. Firstly, I was no longer locked into the drudgery of the production line. Secondly, I felt I was being given the opportunity to pour all my efforts into a working-class organisation. I was no longer just a tool in the great machine of capitalism; I felt, as so many other trade unionists had done, that I was embarking on a crusade to make sure that capitalism worked, as far as possible, for our members. I was sure that at last I would find job satisfaction. Beryl understood my feelings about all of this, and she willingly supported me.

As far as the car industry was concerned, my duties covered only the Pressed Steel plant (another official was responsible for the Morris Motors plant and the car delivery industry, which were both real trouble spots). After working on the line, I knew intimately what each man's working day was like. For fourteen years I had got up at 6.00 a.m. each morning and cycled the six miles to the factory. As I arrived on the outskirts of Cowley, and as I left at night, the road was a wide flowing river of bicycles: there were few cars, because workers in those days could not afford them.

The Pressed Steel factory had been built in the 1920s, and covered an area the size of Hyde Park; it even had its own railway system. At one time there were over 14,000 people working there, and there were seven canteens, strictly segregated for manual workers, white-collar staff, foremen, middle management, senior management, directors and managing directors. Single-status canteens were unheard of.

We had to be ready to start as soon as the works hooter went at 7.15 a.m.; in the 1950s we finished work at 5.15 p.m. with two tea breaks of ten minutes, at 9.00 a.m. and 3.00 p.m., and one hour for lunch at 11.45 a.m. If we worked two hours' overtime we left the plant at 7.30, more than twelve hours later. Everyone had to work at the speed dictated by the production line, which started moving promptly at 7.15 a.m.; by 9.00 a.m. you could not see across the factory floor because of the smoke and lead dust in the air.

Gangs consisted of anything from 25 to 800 men, and all the money earned by the gang was pooled and shared out at the end of the week.

We dreaded being moved from one line to another on a temporary basis, because we would not be familiar with the new job, but would still be expected to keep up with the experienced workers. If we held up the line we would be accused of preventing them from earning their usual piecework rates. It also meant doing a different job using different muscles from usual, so we would then experience a great deal of pain and stiffness for the rest of the week.

Setting piecework rates was always difficult. Each worker, once he had learned the job, was faced with a timekeeper who stood over him with a stop watch while he performed the task. Once the time was taken, a fixed value in money (usually one or two old pence) was placed on each minute. When an agreement was reached it then became 'the rate for the job'. Obviously our main aim was always to maximise the time taken while the timekeeper was there, and minimise the time after he had gone, thus raising our earnings to the maximum possible. That also made it possible to leave the factory as soon as the schedule was completed, whatever the time. I was once rated on a job which the timekeeper observed at forty-five minutes – it was tricky to stretch it out that long, and the timekeeper even joked, 'Wake me up when you've finished.' I knew that if I worked at maximum pace, I could probably do it in five minutes.

Piecework had many drawbacks; one was that it was very hard on older men because of their lower strength and stamina. If I argued that they should be given less arduous jobs, the others would say, 'If they want to earn the same money as us, they must do whatever job is available or get out of the gang.' Piecework did not breed tolerance or compassion among the workforce.

This was the background of experience I brought to my new task as a union official. Those years, together with my time as a shop steward, stood me in good stead. Now mass meetings, hard negotiations with senior management, disputes with other unions, attending difficult branch meetings and explaining complicated deals became part of my everyday routine. I had never been happier and could not believe my luck. I now saw twenty-five years before me of doing a job I believed in.

In the years that followed, the car industry, and especially the plants at Cowley, became famous for industrial disputes, but in fact the two factories were very different. William Morris, the founder of Morris

Motors, was strongly opposed to the presence of unions, and did not want his workers to have recognition or negotiating rights. In the nineteen-twenties, as the first factory in the area, the Morris plant recruited its workers locally, from shops, farms and the Oxford colleges. These manual workers were glad to find jobs which paid slightly more than their previous employment, and with prospects of continuing work in a growing industry, but they had no experience of trade union organisation.

The Pressed Steel plant was built afterwards, to supply Morris Motors with car bodies. Since all the local labour had already been absorbed by Morris, workers were recruited from the north east, Scotland, Wales, Cornwall, and the Yorkshire coal mines. Many of them came from industrial areas and they already had trade union cards and experience – and many of them belonged to the TGWU. The result was that unions were recognised at the Pressed Steel plant as early as 1936. During the 1950s and 1960s, three unions in the Morris plant campaigned hard to recruit members and obtain full trade union rights: these were the TGWU, the AEU (Amalgamated Engineering Unions) and the NUVB (National Union of Vehicle Builders). At Morris these were not recognised until the dispute involving Frank Horsman in 1959, and even then only people employed in the plant were allowed to negotiate. Full-time union officials (who might have a view of the larger picture) were not welcomed.

This attitude of management had some serious consequences at Morris. First, because management believed that to compromise was a sign of weakness, the shop stewards seldom achieved reasonable settlements. Consequently employees with extreme left-wing opinions, who mostly had political rather than trade union objectives, gained ground with the workforce with their promises of taking a stronger line in negotiations. Secondly, because the management excluded full-time union officials, the more militant union stewards were able to operate without any external controls. They continued to belong to the union because they wanted its official backing and protection, but they did not want the duties and responsibilities that came with membership to interfere with their activities. In effect, they were operating a union within a union, and with the help of the management they continued to do this for several years.

My first real test came during 1966, in a dispute in the Morris plant over bonus pay. An unofficial one-day strike had been called, and eight men had ignored it. This was in the early days of militancy, when certain shop stewards wanted to demonstrate to the workers what they could achieve if they had their support. The eight men were called to a mass meeting and asked to give an undertaking to honour strike decisions in the future. The meeting took place on company premises and the 'strike breakers' had been standing under a gantry; during the proceedings someone threw a rope over this to make it look like a gallows. Someone reported this to a journalist and the next day the *Daily Mirror* ran a headline saying 'Workers tried under a hanging noose'. As this was the first day of the 1966 General Election campaign the Conservative press made the most of it. Quentin Hogg, later Lord Chancellor, wrote in the *Daily Express*,

> I find it impossible to believe that this really happened in Britain, Oxford, England, which I have known and loved all my life ... Responsibility rests squarely with the Prime Minister, as leader of the Labour Party. His party is financed and controlled by the unions.

The TGWU official responsible for the Morris plant was away on holiday, so it became my responsibility: I was instructed by Jack Jones to bring the dispute to an end. I attended a branch meeting of about 300 members with a message from the General Executive of the union that the strike should be called off with a promise of negotiations with the management. I was astonished by the hostility I met there. The formal response was, 'We propose that the TGWU Executive and Brother Buckle go and fuck themselves – the strike goes on.'

I was a very inexperienced official and it was the first genuinely angry meeting I had faced; I wondered whether I should walk out and give in, or stand my ground and fight. Although I was very nervous, I stayed on and continued to argue my case. It was important that the members allowed me to start negotiations, even if that meant calling off the strike. And more importantly, the trade union movement should not give the Tory press vital ammunition with which to attack the Labour movement in the early stages of an election campaign. In the end, much to my surprise, I carried my point and the recommendation was accepted. I left the meeting feeling immensely relieved that the ordeal was over, only to be met by a crowd of press reporters and a TV camera crew wanting interviews. I began to realise that my new job had placed me at the focus of a great deal of public attention.

I learned a lot from that experience, both about the attentions of the press and also about the difficulties of dealing with my own union members. Often the negotiations with management were relatively simple, compared with the task of achieving a united front among the workers.

An example was the situation which arose when the Pressed Steel management wanted to change the grade structure. This structure had been in place since the 1930s, with some forty or fifty different pay grades in place within the plant; they wanted to replace these with only seven grades. The TGWU felt that the company favoured the skilled men and the craft unions above the others: in the opinion of the management, unskilled labour was less important because it was always available. The result was that all the unions disagreed among themselves. We ended up with a major conference at which our differences became so evident that the management suggested an adjournment so that we could sort ourselves out. At one point the arguments were so heated that John Boyd, General Secretary of the AEU and a staunch Salvation Army man, said, 'Brothers, can I suggest we have five minutes of quiet contemplation and pray to God for guidance and advice?' The TGWU senior steward, Josh Murphy, replied, 'And which union does he belong to?' It took several further meetings before the issue was eventually settled with a new time-workers' pay structure.

During the 1960s it became clear that the British motor industry was in decline: economic changes such as inflation and devaluation, changes in government-controlled systems such as road tax and petrol taxes, and the growth of foreign manufacturers had all had an effect on the British market. In an attempt to save the industry a series of mergers took place, culminating in that of Leyland Motors and British Motor Holdings (which included by then both Pressed Steel Fisher and Austin-Morris) into the British Leyland Motor Corporation. Meanwhile another company, the Rootes Group, had stopped placing any work with Pressed Steel: the loss of independence meant that they did not want to risk their commercial secrets being known by rival companies.

The management of British Leyland was under pressure to make a success of this new venture, and in 1969 a new model, the Marina, was introduced. This was intended to replace the work lost from Rootes, which had caused great hardship in short-time working. At the same time the management announced that they would end the piecework system, a decision which would have far-reaching effects on conditions of employment within the plant. Workers valued it because it gave them some control over their working day; for similar reasons management disliked it because they felt it denied them total control over earnings.

Once again I found myself involved in a major dispute. Luckily I had worked the piecework system for fourteen years, so I understood its weaknesses: it encouraged men to accept poor working conditions in order to achieve increased earnings; older people were excluded from the gang if they failed to keep up the pace; short-time working was common; jobs were insecure; and sudden mass redundancies could be imposed. Its one strength was that it gave the workers some participation in decisions and protected them from total management control, and for this reason they resisted its removal.

The management exhorted the workers to respond to this change in a responsible manner, but they themselves resorted to industrial blackmail: they said that if the piecework system remained in place the Marina would not be produced at Cowley. This was the last straw for workers already demoralised by a long period of short-time working, and morale was very low. When management announced that they were introducing a new system of Measured Daywork, which gave them total control over pay, there seemed no alternative but acceptance.

Personally I was happy to see the end of piecework, but I knew we had to salvage something. It was at this point that I intervened with a compromise: in December 1970 I devised a system called 'Mutuality'. This said that if the company wished to increase line speeds, add or remove workers from the line, or change methods of working, mutual agreement must be reached between employment and management before any changes were made. This reflected the kind of controls we had a right to under piecework. I discussed my ideas with our senior shop steward Bill Roche, an astute and experienced man with a much sharper brain than mine. When he accepted the general principles I felt confident to go further, but I knew I needed support from a senior level in the union, because the management were currently in such a strong bargaining position. Although it was not usual for the General Secretary to meet District Secretaries on such matters, Jack Jones agreed to see me and gave me his support.

This proved a wise move. Initially the management were horrified at my suggestions for clawing back some control for the workforce over their conditions, but when I told them that I had the full support of my General Secretary, they changed their tone. Our conference was attended by Bill Roche, the senior shop steward, Alec Morton, the Branch Secretary, and Revd Tony Williamson, the Branch Chairman. Moss Evans, then the TGWU National Secretary for the Automotive Industry, often joked that management did not have a chance: they were negotiating with 'three magistrates and a bloody parson!' After sixty-six hours of intense negotiations during January 1971 we were ready to report to the members. At a mass meeting of five thousand workers I explained the terms of the mutuality document; it was accepted and became the first of its kind in the industry. Both management and unions understood that mutuality did not mean saying 'no' to every proposal from either side, but rather 'discuss and reach an agreement in the best interests of everyone'.

The agreement meant that every worker received £42 per week for a guaranteed forty hours. No longer was there any cause to remove fellow workers from the line because of age, and disputes between members ended. Mutuality lasted for nine years without any major disputes, until it was abolished by a new, harsher breed of management under Michael Edwardes.

As a result of the mutuality agreement, which established a basic wage for a forty-hour week, some of the skilled men started to demand a higher hourly rate, but the union resisted this – contrary to popular opinion, our union was not in the business of pushing for more money all the time, but rather of working in the best interests of all the workforce. We in the union did not feel that the skilled craftsmen should have higher wages for several reasons. First, the unskilled men actually worked harder: the skilled men could work at their own pace, but the production workers were driven by the speed of the line; secondly, in spite of the guaranteed week, the skilled men still had more job security and were able to command more overtime; and thirdly, although the skilled men earned less during their apprenticeship, their earning power then increased sharply and remained high right to the end of their working life – the production workers, on the other hand, were often taken off the line when they could no longer keep up, and so their income dropped.

At this point we launched our campaign in the Cowley Body plant, with the inspired title (thought up by Bill Roche) of 'Second to None'. It encapsulated in its slogan what we wanted to achieve: the same hourly rate for both skilled and semi-skilled employees. Once again we were successful and that agreement too stayed in place until 1981 when it was removed by the same management team.

In spite of these achievements, the motor industry was still perceived as a hotbed of dissent and industrial dispute. Foreign manufacturers were still making increasing inroads into our traditional markets, and the 1973 oil crisis sent the whole industry into shock. In 1974 the Secretary of Trade and Industry, Tony Benn, appointed Sir Don Ryder to conduct a detailed enquiry into the whole company. When the report was published the following year it pointed out that BL had some 170,000 employees divided between 60 plants, 8 divisions and 17 unions; this produced 52 separate bargaining units. The proposal was that the system of bargaining should be centralised. I could see many problems inherent in national bargaining, but at least my life would become simpler: I would no longer have to prepare and bargain annual pay reviews for each local unit individually.

By 1976, years of failure by management to provide good working conditions, adequate investment, or even to produce the planned new models had at last caught up with British Leyland; this was all revealed by the Ryder Report. Long before, in 1971, the *Sunday Times* Business Section had reported,

> The collapse of BL's profits from £40m to £3m marks the most important management failure in British industry over the last three years. No efforts to blame the unions, the government or the legacy of the distant past can conceal this fact.

The real seeds of trouble had been sown much earlier by William Morris, who seemed more concerned with his philanthropic activities than with the wellbeing of his workforce. He gave huge and very welcome donations to the Oxford hospitals, and ensured that Nuffield College was built bearing his name, but he failed to invest in new technology or good working conditions. I once suggested in a lecture I gave at Nuffield College that there should be a brass plate on the door saying 'This college was endowed at the expense of Lord Nuffield's low-paid workers and the future of his company.'

The crisis we faced was due to a management failure of the first magnitude; no one had anticipated or planned for the emergence of foreign car manufacturers. The industries in Japan, Germany and Italy had recovered from the effects of the last war and were now invading our market share at an alarming rate.

By 1976 BL's mounting financial problems had come to a head: an expensive investment programme was needed if the company was to remain competitive, but the banks refused to invest and it was not possible to raise the money on the Stock Exchange. BL had to turn to the government's National Enterprise Board for funding. Jack Jones and Hugh Scanlon called a meeting of all the senior officials of the TGWU and AEU in London, to present us with an ultimatum. They had met the Prime Minister, Jim Callaghan, that morning, and been told that the government would not make any further cash available to the company until our two unions gave assurances that industrial unrest was at an end, and the militants would be brought under control.

Our first reaction was exasperation. For years Jack Jones had told us that the shop stewards were the workers' real representatives, and that the full-time officials were there only to carry out their wishes. Now he was telling us that in order to ensure the continuation of the company we had to take a long-term view and if necessary oppose the wishes of the shop stewards. It was a dramatic change of stance, giving us an insight into the depth of the crisis. In the end we all agreed to do everything we could to keep the industrial peace and thus qualify for government support. We realised that in order to save the company both Jack Jones and Hugh Scanlon were being forced to ask us and our shop stewards to adopt policies totally opposed to their and our belief in worker involvement.

In fact, in my experience the vast majority of shop stewards were very responsible people, and needed no lectures from me; it was only a small handful of politically motivated stewards, such as those in the Cowley Assembly plant, who were constantly calling strikes for ridiculous reasons and generally baiting the management at every opportunity. There was now no doubt about it: a storm was brewing at a national level for the militants.

Throughout the 1970s the militants had become an increasing problem within the unions. They managed to gain influence partly because the management were initially reluctant to make concessions in any negotiations, and excluded the full-time union officials as much as possible. Workers began to support the militants not because they accepted their political dogma, but because they hoped and believed that only left-wing stewards could obtain improvements from a hard-line management. Later on this actually began to happen, because during the 1960s and 1970s, when the militants called for repeated strikes, management were desperate to achieve continuous production, and would then concede almost anything rather than have a stoppage on the line. This vacillating management style did nothing to produce a consistent relationship of trust between workers and their managers.

Things ran more smoothly in the Pressed Steel plant partly because of the different union style there. The TGWU had a system whereby no gang could strike without first reporting their dispute to a full shop stewards' meeting. If the meeting supported them, they could go ahead with union action and the management would know that they were, in effect, faced with action by the whole membership. If support from the other stewards was not forthcoming, no dispute would take place. This system of collective action worked well for many years, and meant that there were comparatively few strikes at Pressed Steel. At the Assembly plant across the road in one year there were over five hundred strikes, lasting between ten minutes and three weeks; in another year over a thousand separate claims were tabled for increased pay.

The militants in the Assembly plant had a range of tactics calculated to maximise disruption. They would often call a mass meeting of members and seek support for a strike on an issue of pay or working conditions. When the vote was taken they would note those who voted against taking action. They would single out those members and tell them to return to work, before taking a second vote; they could then report to the management that they had received a unanimous vote in support of their claim. When the strike started they would tell the dissenters that their work would be 'blacked' (not touched by anyone else) unless they supported the strike.

One of the best-known stewards was Alan Thornett, a member of the Workers' Socialist League and the Workers' Revolutionary Party. He would call a small group of employees to a meeting in a public part of the plant and say, 'All those in favour of a pay rise please show,' indicating a show of hands. Naturally everyone was in favour of more pay in principle – there was never any discussion of the long-term implications of such random claims – and he would then tell the management that he had a unanimous vote in favour of a pay claim, without mentioning the numbers involved. Once a claim was tabled in this way, and a 'Failure to agree' had been recorded, it was my job to take the claim further: usually this was an impossible task, as there was no real case to put, and we would be easily defeated by the management.

When I asked him why he continually did this, starting actions he had no hope of winning, he replied,

'The workers must go down to one defeat after another until they learn to become revolutionaries.'

'But that means that management can have one victory after another at the workers' expense,' I answered. 'That's not what I'm here for.'

This was true; all I ever wanted was the best deal for my members, who were so often the victims in a huge game of power politics and high finance. All they wanted was a fair wage and job security in exchange for their hard, boring and dangerous work.

In the summer of 1977 the union official in charge of the Assembly plant retired, and Jack Jones asked me if I would take over union responsibility for the whole of the car industry in the Oxford District. I knew that this would mean taking on the militants, and I warned him that there would be 'blood on the shop floor'. It would not be an easy task. Jack assured me that provided I did not breach union policy or the union rule book, and did nothing illegal, I would have his full support.

He kept his word. To the end of my time at Cowley the militants and I had a constant battle, and they were forever sending resolutions to the General Secretary calling for my removal; delegations of disgruntled stewards would call on Jack Jones in his office to complain about me, but to no avail.

Much to the anger of the militants my first act was to introduce secret ballots for the elections of shop stewards. The previous system had been self-perpetuating, as the senior steward and his deputies were elected by other stewards and not by the wider membership. When the first ballot was held, the militants thought that they should organise it, but I brought in thirty impartial shop stewards from outside the industry, and they ran the ballot. As a result, nearly all the militants lost their positions and more reasonable people were elected.

I had to resort to other manipulative tactics to defeat their activities. When the militant members began to disrupt District Committee meetings to the extent that no business could be done, I was asked to change the Standing Orders in such a way as to enable us to work. I rewrote them to say that 75% of all known delegates constituted a quorum. If at any time attendance at a meeting fell below this 75%, the chairman would close the meeting and all further business would be lost. We then placed all left-wing non-union motions at the end of the agenda. This meant that if the militants became disruptive we could arrange for some of our delegates to leave the meeting; as the meeting would then close, the militant motions would never be discussed or voted on. They soon realised that they would lose either way: if they caused trouble the meeting ended; if they behaved themselves, unacceptable motions were then defeated by the moderatè majority. This curbed their more disruptive tactics.

I was determined that they should not beat us. After a while, many of the workers began to see that the militants could be a greater threat to their job security than the management; at that point they began to turn against them, and stopped supporting silly claims and taking strike action at the slightest pretence. It was too late. I had warned the militants on several occasions that if they continued with their strategies a more hard-line management would be brought in to deal with them, and in 1977 that was what happened. Michael Edwardes was appointed Chairman of British Leyland, and a new and unpleasant era for unions began.

When he was appointed, Edwardes said, 'I know nothing about how to make cars, but I will do my best to make the company successful.' In my view he proved himself right on the first point; I am not sure about the second. In 1978 he addressed all the union officials and told us how he planned to save the company. At the end of his speech, Derek Robinson (the AEU senior shop steward at Longbridge) proposed a vote of support for the new Chairman: I was one of only five who voted against. I felt sure that Edwardes did not believe in consensus, and that he planned to ride roughshod over everyone. Time proved me right: within three years he had imposed a national grade structure, grade rates and an incentive scheme; working practices which swept away forty years of trade union democracy. All employees were told that if they attended work on a certain day in April 1981 they would be deemed to have accepted their new conditions; if they failed to report for work they would be deemed to have dismissed themselves. This was the new authoritarian style of management which we were facing.

How much of this was due to Edwardes' personal style, and how much was forced upon him by his political masters remains unknown. I spent a lot of time in the early 1980s being interviewed by the press, radio and television, since industrial disputes continued at Cowley and they became the focus of media interest. Sometimes I had to explain why strikes were happening, and at others I had the opportunity to criticise Edwardes' harsh management techniques. Eventually he wrote to me, saying that it was people like me who were preventing him from making BL successful, and inviting me to meet him at his private office.

The meeting was a curious one: it was not usual for chairmen of industry to meet district officials, so it had to be kept secret. He started the meeting by treating me to a furious tirade about my conduct and the things I was saying and writing about him in the press. I sat through this in silence, and when he finally slowed down, I pointed out that I had not been employed by the company for some years.

'I'm not one of your terrified managers, so I'm not afraid of you. Now can we have a civilised discussion?'

I then listed the matters I wanted to discuss: his style of management, his decision to close the MG factory at Abingdon, and his refusal to honour the results of management/union ballots when he lost them.

Curiously, he seemed surprised when I reminded him of some of the circumstances of the MG closure. He seemed not to know that employees had been told that if they resisted closure they would be dismissed for misconduct and lose their redundancy entitlement; if, on the other hand, they co-operated, they would be given extra. In effect, they had been blackmailed with their own redundancy pay. He was also surprised when I told him about the excellent history of the MG plant's good industrial relations and productivity. It was at that point that he referred to his 'political masters' who had caused him to close the plant.

At the end of our meeting we had reached no agreement. I had little sympathy with his position: whatever the political pressures, all these management actions were done in his name, and it was his business to know about them. It happened to be my birthday that day, and as I left, he offered me a large cream cake, to make up for the fact that a family gathering had had to be cancelled to fit into his schedule. I refused politely, but he clearly could not understand why I would not leave his office with his gift of a cream cake under my arm: industrial psychology was not one of his strong points.

There was one action for which I will praise Edwardes: the deal he made between BL and the Japanese company Honda. I had high hopes that at last a company which did know something about producing cars would ensure BL's future. When the first contingent of Japanese engineers were due to arrive, the management asked me how the workforce was likely to react. I suggested that the first thing they should do was to find out if there were any ex-prisoners of war among them, veterans of the war in the Far East, and warn them first. We found that there were twenty-eight such men, and we spoke to them all separately: no problems developed. When the first consignment of Japanese car parts arrived, one of the shop stewards rang to tell me what the quality was like.

'The men were given crowbars to open the crates,' he said, 'and they refused to use them. The containers were so well made, they didn't want to damage them!' It was a good omen. He went on, 'Dave, the car parts actually fit first time' – a rare event at Cowley in those days.

I knew then that Edwardes had got something right. At the Cowley Body plant today the effects of that Japanese deal can be seen everywhere: up-to-date tooling, good facilities, clean and quiet working conditions: things we begged for in vain in the 1950s and 1960s.

Typical of Edwardes' methods was the national wage bargaining dispute in 1981, when the annual wage claim could not be agreed. All the parties went to London to the Advisory, Conciliation and Arbitration Service (ACAS) headquarters on a Saturday morning; a strike involving the whole company was due to start on the Monday. The whole BL negotiating team was there, including General Secretaries of most unions and Len Murray of the TUC; the management side was represented by Edwardes and his senior team. The idea was that ACAS should arbitrate between the different parties.

However, impartiality was not the order of the day. Early that morning Edwardes was interviewed on national radio, saying that if the meeting failed to reach an agreement and a strike took place, he had the authority of the government to say that the company would be closed down. If the unions had made such a threat prior to such critical negotiations it would have been described as 'threat and intimidation', and I believe that ACAS should have objected; however, the new chairman of ACAS was Pat Lowry, until recently BL's Director of Personnel, a man partly responsible for the policies which had brought about the dispute.

In the event, we local officials were effectively excluded from the negotiations, being kept in a separate room while ACAS officials went from one to another informing us of what each side wished to say. It was not my idea of genuine collective bargaining or effective communication. In the end it was clear that the national officials had reached an agreement without consulting the local officials, who were merely told that they must go back to their districts and inform mass meetings that they must call off the strike and accept the deal. The workforce were not happy with this either, but they knew that if the national union leaders would not support them , there was no chance of an official strike.

This whole experience proved one thing to me: national bargaining serves the interests of both management and national union leaders, and fails too often to take account of local conditions and local aspirations.

Industrial relations reached a particularly low point during Edwardes' time: many managers began to treat the unions with real contempt. There was one instance when a spontaneous strike took place in the Cowley plant and a senior steward went out to calm things down. He advised everyone to return to work, saying that he knew how unreasonable management were, but he would try to resolve matters. Unfortunately his remarks were reported in the local paper, and he was disciplined for making hostile remarks about the management. He was given a final written warning and told that if it happened again he would be sacked – and he was a man who had worked in the industry for forty years with an unblemished record.

In an attempt to speak in his defence, I obtained a formal interview with the plant Personnel Manager. We had hardly begun when the door burst open and a senior plant manager walked in.

'Why are you wasting your fucking time on bastards like him?' he asked the Personnel Manager. I explained why we were meeting and asked him to leave us to talk in peace. He refused, saying to the Personnel Manager, 'Why don't you get off your arse and do some useful fucking work?' He also made similar remarks to me. I demanded an apology and eventually obtained it, but the written warning was not withdrawn. This was the kind of response we frequently met in those days.

In his book *Back from the Brink*, Michael Edwardes wrote

> We needed to re-establish management authority, both outside the company, where our management of material purchasing was lacking in discipline, and inside the company where our 198,000 employees were relatively leaderless.
>
> To regain the management role would mean counteracting shop steward power, which had got out of hand to the point where national union leaders, local union officials, and certainly management, were being treated in a cavalier fashion by some 200 militant stewards who had filled the vacuum left by management ...
>
> The objective was not to destroy or weaken unions. On the contrary, it was to rebalance the whole order of things so that together with management national union officials would be able to play a proper role without finding their authority eroded by strong stewards, weak management, and lack of understanding of what management was trying to achieve.

In 1983 I was invited by the *New Socialist* magazine to review Edwardes' book. At the time I was involved in a major dispute at Cowley which had largely arisen over his style of management, so the invitation came at a good time. I wrote,

> The company expects, and rightly so, a high quality product. The employee is equally entitled to a quality of life. My real criticism of the Edwardes era is that he put commercial success above human needs; but surely there has to be a balance. If not, modern industry is turning people into robots, and no one should complain if they revolt.
>
> Sir Michael may have thought the crisis he inherited justified an authoritarian industrial relations system, but a different style is required now – more open, trusting and democratic.

When Michael Edwardes left the company in 1982 he was mourned by few. He had reduced the workforce from 198,000 to 90,000, and of 34 plants he had closed 14. Production had been halved even though new models had been launched; BL's market share in Britain was below 15% and it had an even smaller share of export markets. Edwardes may have known nothing about making cars; he scarcely demonstrated much more knowledge of the secret of success.

The legacy of Edwardes' years at BL was deep resentment and suspicion of management on the part of the workforce. This was demonstrated during my last major dispute at Cowley. Since 1946 workers had had the right to wash their hands at the end of the morning and afternoon shifts, and thus this had become 'custom and practice'. A senior Director visiting the plant saw men leaving the line three minutes early at lunchtime, and ordered that the practice should be stopped at once. We tried through all the usual procedures to claim this right but the management were adamant: we were told that when workers reported for duty on the following Monday they would be 'deemed to have accepted that the six minutes washing-up time had ceased and was no longer a right.' On the Monday morning 5,000 workers walked out and the plant was empty within thirty minutes. What became known as the 'washing-up dispute' had begun and was to last four weeks. In many ways it symbolised the pent-up anger among the workers over the arbitrary decisions and actions of the managers.

Once again the negotiations were protracted; at one stage I had a stand-up argument with Moss Evans, who was very ill at the time, and who ordered me to produce a formula to resolve the dispute. When I refused, saying that I had already done so, he threatened to sack me from the union, although he later apologised. He was anxious to achieve a conclusion: it was estimated that the strike lost the company around £150m, and each worker was believed to have lost about £500 in wages despite receiving strike pay.

At the height of the dispute I summed up the feelings of many BL employees by saying in an interview, 'If the price of economic success is a system of industrial slavery, that is too high a price for working people to pay.' The use of that emotive word 'slavery' struck the right chord with the press, who on the whole were very sympathetic; I had been afraid they would ridicule the cause of the strike. The other issue in the dispute was the company's authoritarian attitude towards its employees. I have always challenged the dogma, 'Management has a right to manage.' My belief is that 'Management has a duty to manage humanely.' The strike ended with a partial victory for the union, and the six minutes' washing-up time each day was retained for some time.

There were many problems during those turbulent years, which encompassed the rise of the militant unions and also that of Thatcherite industrialism. As a union official I did not see it as my duty to encourage every wage-claim and complaint brought to me – hence my frequent opposition to the militants. I did see it as my duty to represent the best interests of the workers, whether in the areas of pay, working conditions or safety.

The latter years at BL were marked by developments which placed power in the hands of the management: from the 1968 formation of the British Leyland Motor Corporation there had been several landmark events. First, the abandonment of piecework and the introduction of Measured Daywork; then the Ryder Report and the first move towards centralised bargaining; then the arrival of Michael Edwardes in 1977; the Edwardes plan and the use of ballots linked with a disregard of normal consultation procedures; and the imposition of new working practices and local agreements without genuine negotiations. All of these developments made life harder for those of us who tried to use the formal channels to work together with management. I am not sure the trade union movement ever found the answers needed to protect our members in the manner we wished, or they were entitled to.

I spent the 1970s resisting the extreme left within the union, and the 1980s resisting the extreme right among the management. From 1979 when the Conservatives came into power BL was turned into a test bed for the government's economic and industrial relations theories. Michael Edwardes was a willing partner in that cause, and I saw those policies as deeply damaging to everything the trade unions had ever fought for and won.

By 1992 the Assembly plant had been closed and all car production concentrated in the Body plant; the workforce was reduced to 4,500. A vast area of wasteland exists where the factories once stood, and small business parks and light industries are springing up in their place. It is a microcosm of what befell so much of Britain's manufacturing industry over the last twenty years.

8. Another Life

All through my working life at Cowley I was conscious that I seemed to be living another life in parallel. For one thing, there was my work as a magistrate: it was informed and affected by my experiences as a shop steward and a trade union negotiator (indeed, chairing a bench between two other magistrates in mutual disagreement over a case sometimes required similar skills) but the dignified atmosphere of the court was a world apart from the noise and dirt of factory life. Then, as time went on, I was also invited to join several other bodies.

Over the years I had become increasingly interested in the whole issue of race relations. Oxford, like many other manufacturing areas, had seen an increase in the number of immigrants arriving from both Asia and the West Indies – nowadays about 3% of the population consists of minority ethnic groups – and many of them sought jobs in the transport and car manufacturing industries. I often used to hear shop stewards referring to 'those black bastards taking our jobs', and this offended me. Of course, any threat, whether real or imagined, to the availability of jobs alarmed the working man. When Enoch Powell made his infamous 'rivers of blood' speech in 1968, the next day thousands of dockers marched through London in support, and they were mostly TGWU members. Many of us in the trade union movement were concerned at the divisiveness of such prejudice in our society.

During April 1967 I was invited by Mark Bonham Carter, the Chairman of the Race Relations Board, to a meeting with him and John

Little, the Chief Executive. They asked me to become a member of the West Metropolitan Conciliation Committee, which dealt with complaints about racial prejudice, and I accepted; I was to work on that committee for nine years. When the Race Relations Act was passed in 1976, the Conciliation Committees were abolished, and all complaints were dealt with by Industrial Tribunals. I was then appointed as a member of the National Tribunal system for the Oxford area, sitting in Reading. On the whole trade unionists were appointed to these tribunals through their unions, and employers were appointed through the CBI. I was an unusual case, since I was regarded as something of a specialist in race relations work, and so was invited simply to transfer from the Conciliation Committee to the Tribunal. We dealt with a wide range of complaints about prejudice in the workplace, such as employers operating unofficial quota systems, ethnic minorities failing to achieve promotions, or sackings for racial reasons rather than industrial misconduct.

At first I was worried that the Tribunals would be less thorough than the Conciliation Committees in their dealing with matters of race, and to some extent this was so. A classic case occurred just before I was appointed to the Tribunal, so that my involvement was still that of a trade union negotiator. A man named Ashraf, who worked on the production line at the Assembly plant, successfully applied for three months' leave of absence from his job to visit his dying mother in Pakistan. He was required by the management to sign an undertaking that he would return on the due date; failure to do so would mean that he had left the company voluntarily. In the event he did indeed fail to return to work, but only because he was suffering from dysentery and unable to travel. His illness was properly certificated by a doctor, who thought that he might have contracted the disease because after living for many years in Britain, he was no longer used to drinking the local water or eating the local food in Pakistan.

On his eventual return he was told that he had lost his job, and I represented him at the Industrial Tribunal at which I claimed he had been unfairly dismissed. When I raised the issue of the cause of his illness, the Chairman interrupted me to say,

'What nonsense, Mr Buckle. *These people* only eat chapattis and rice.' I objected to his comments but was overruled. Some time later I noticed that another member of the Tribunal had dozed off to sleep; I continued making my case and allowed her to sleep on for a while. Then I addressed the Chairman directly.

'On a point of order, Mr Chairman, I should like to request that this hearing is adjourned and a new Tribunal set up. My reasons are that firstly, by your remarks you have demonstrated a clear prejudice against the immigrant community, and secondly, that your colleague on your right is fast asleep and has been so for at least half an hour.' The hearing was stopped; at a subsequent hearing I won the case. This was what lay behind my doubts about the ability of Industrial Tribunals to make a good job of race relations cases. (This particular case had an odd history. British Leyland afterwards appealed and won their case, so my success was overturned. Twelve months later I happened to attend another Tribunal in London and heard one of the lawyers BL had used appearing in a similar case, but for the defence, pleading exactly the same points that I had made, and he won his case. The Ashraf matter had become case law. When I tackled him over his change of position he merely smiled and said, 'Well, that's the law for you.')

It was not always easy for someone of my background to move in such different circles. When I had been a magistrate for some years, I received an invitation to a Garden Party at Buckingham Palace. Initially I had no intention of attending: as a lifelong Labour supporter I did not have much time for such Establishment 'treats'. However, Beryl put me in my place. 'David, don't be selfish,' she said. 'The invitation is addressed to both of us, and I *would* like to go. I'd like to see what a Garden Party is like, and I'd like to see inside the grounds of Buckingham Palace.' So I accepted, and on the appointed day we dressed up in our best and set off.

When we arrived and walked around, I realised that I recognised lots of other magistrates, so clearly it was an invitation that had been sent out to magistrates in the Oxfordshire area. One magistrate whom I knew very well approached us. He was very smartly dressed in a morning suit (as were many of the others) and said,

'Well, David, fancy seeing you here, of all people! I am surprised. But I see you're wearing a lounge suit. You're not in proper morning dress.'

Quick as a flash Beryl spoke up and said, 'No, he's not. But he is probably one of the very few men here today who actually owns the clothes he's wearing!'

Beryl's mother Eve, who was a dear soul now in her late seventies, had been absolutely thrilled when she heard we were going to the Palace, and she asked us to bring her back a cake. So when we went to the marquee for our tea and cakes we explained what we wanted, and collected a cake for Eve wrapped up in a napkin. We took it home for her, and she was tickled pink with it! Eve had been sent into service as a kitchen maid at the age of thirteen, and she had spent most of her life in the service of the rich and the powerful. To her it was wonderful that she should have a cake that came from Buckingham Palace itself.

In 1978 I received a letter from Hugh Jenkins, the Labour Minister for the Arts, inviting me to become a member of the Arts Council of Great Britain and Northern Ireland. I readily accepted, though not without a great deal of doubt in my mind about whether I was competent. There was no indication of what would be involved. I was met by the Chairman, Kenneth Robinson, and he and a group of the other members asked me a series of questions about my involvement with the arts. I am sure that they must have thought I was not very bright, because I had only a general interest in the arts, rather than an intellectual one. My interest had been stimulated by my friends Arturo and Ilsa Burea, and developed by my visits to art galleries, concerts and performances, but I had learned the hard way, by reading and experience rather than by a liberal education.

I was very surprised at the way the Arts Council did its business. At my second meeting, the agenda was suddenly interrupted by the Chairman who said,

'Oh, by the way, there's something I forgot to put on the agenda. The Secretary General and I thought it would be a good idea to buy a shop. There's one for sale behind Covent Garden, and it would be an ideal place for the Council to sell its books. We've both been to see it, and it costs £87,000. Is everybody agreed?'

All around the table heads were nodding in agreement. I was the only person to raise an objection, albeit rather timidly.

'Excuse me, Chairman,' I said, 'but is this the usual way we do business? Surely we need to have an architect's report and a surveyor's report, and we ought to go and see these premises before committing so much money.'

'Oh, no, Mr Buckle,' came the airy reply. 'That's the way we usually do things around this table.'

I formed the opinion, rightly or wrongly, that most of the members of the committee saw their appointment as a status symbol, and were merely yes-men and -women. They were impressed by the power of being on this prestigious Establishment quango, and did not want to do or say anything disruptive, in spite of the carefree way in which taxpayers' money was being spent.

I was on the Council when the Conservatives came into power. The new minister, Norman St John Stevas, attended our first meeting after the election, and gave a lucid presentation of his aims. I knew that many local authorities had been putting money into local arts projects, and I asked him whether, if cuts were made in local authority funding, central government would make up the difference for the arts.

'Most certainly not,' he replied. 'If you think local government and the arts have had a difficult time in the past, it's nothing to the hurricane that's about to hit them.'

I had been expecting such an answer, and I produced a pamphlet published by him before the election, which said that the Conservatives 'would not be involved in candle-end economies' for the arts.

This was met with a scowl. 'What's written before an election and what happens afterwards are two different stories,' was his response. Marghanita Laski, who happened to be sitting next to me, knew that it was not the accepted practice to make implied criticisms of the government. She turned to me and murmured, 'Well, that's you off the Council at the first opportunity, David.'

Some time later, at another meeting, we were told the sum allocated to the Arts Council by the government's 'parliamentary grant-in-aid' for that year, but the announcement was followed immediately by the information that 72% of this had already been allocated 'in accordance with past custom and practice', which did not leave much for the Council to decide. As usual I had a few questions to ask, one about why so little (1%) was given to literature – the reply was that the Council felt that 1% was sufficient because of the existence of public libraries. My other question was about music, and in particular, whether the Council gave any subsidies to brass bands. There was a moment's silence, and then one member repeated in horrified tones rather like Lady Bracknell's, *'Brass bands?'* Another member cut in.

'Here at the Arts Council we are concerned with the high arts, not brass bands.'

I am pleased to say that nowadays the Council does indeed fund brass bands.

Appointments to the Council were initially for three years, though members could be reinstated for a further term. One day in 1981 I went along as usual, and sat next to the Chairman at the lunch which routinely preceded the Council meeting. We chatted quite amiably and he said nothing to make me think that anything out of the ordinary was going to happen. Afterwards we walked down to the council chamber together. The agenda always began with an item called 'Chairman's announcements', and on this occasion the Chairman mentioned one or two matters. Then he went on to say,

'I think the Council should know that this is David Buckle's last meeting. Thank you for all your work on behalf of the Council. Next business!' And that was the ignominious end of my time on the Arts Council. Marghanita Laski had been right. I imagine I would have been asked to leave anyway: I was not able to make the kind of contribution I would have liked – I simply did not have the education and I never felt that I was among a peer group. I had often been criticised by friends in the trade union movement for accepting the appointment in the first place, but I had insisted that working class people ought to have a voice on such bodies, and trade unionists should work to represent them wherever they could. However, in the end I didn't make a very good job of that representation: often there were things I wanted to say but I was afraid of making a fool of myself, so I kept silent. I did have one or two supporters on the Council, such as Richard Hoggart and Melvyn Bragg, but on the whole I must admit that I seldom took a full part in the discussions at the Arts Council: I was out of my depth intellectually and I knew it.

Shortly after my appointment to the Arts Council I received a letter from *Who's Who*, the list of public figures in the UK, inviting me to compile my entry to the publication. I replied with a polite refusal, saying that if I had been invited for listing before my appointment to the Arts Council, I would have accepted, but that I did not feel that my work on the Council alone merited my inclusion. In private I felt that the other work I had been doing for years was much more important to society than sitting for a brief period on this committee whose work was performed so casually. It seemed a typical piece of British snobbery that quiet work behind the scenes always went unnoticed, but that appointment to prestigious public bodies produced recognition.

Another result of that appointment was that the BBC invited me to take part in a series on Radio Three with the rather sexist title of *Man of Action*. It was rather like *Desert Island Discs*, in that it consisted of talking about one's life and experiences, accompanied by a choice of favourite records – only since this was Radio Three it was rather more highbrow and wordy and longer: I had to plan a seventy-five-minute programme. I couldn't resist the invitation, mainly because I had never been inside a radio studio, and I was longing to look round the BBC record library!

In the event it was the hardest thing I have ever done. There was no interviewer to help me along: I had to write the entire script alone and add the records of my choice. Two of them were recordings of the spoken word: Henry's speech before Agincourt from Shakespeare's *Henry V*, and Martin Luther King's famous speech 'I have a dream'. When I arrived at the studio for the recording, the producer, Piers Burton Page, queried my choice of Martin Luther King on the grounds that it was not music, and that he suspected it of being political! I had been prepared for this, and pointed out that no one seemed concerned at the inclusion of Shakespeare, which was also not music. He conceded the point and I was allowed to keep my choice; its 'political' nature was not referred to again. In fact its inclusion was very important to me, because of my involvement in race relations issues; together with Nelson Mandela, Martin Luther King was very much one of my heroes.

During my years as a trade union negotiator at the troubled Cowley car factories, I began to have quite a high profile in the media, since I was always being interviewed on radio and television about this or that strike action. As a result I was noticed by two organisations who both invited me to join them. The first was the Industrial Society, headed at that time by their dynamic director, the late John Garnett (whom I once described as the 'Billy Graham of British industrial relations'). I remained a member of the Executive Committee of that organisation for twelve years, and I am still a member of their council. The other group was the Industrial Participation Association, an organisation concerned, like the Industrial Society, with improving the well-being of working people. Additionally this group worked to improve communication between unions and management, and between management and employees. During my seven years at the IPA I was a member of the working party which drew up a document aimed at improving the whole system of negotiations and communications between employers and unions. It was subsequently accepted by the European Commission as a model for this kind of activity.

As a member of the Industrial Society I often attended functions at the headquarters in London, and one occasion our Patron, the Duke of Edinburgh, attended and we were presented to him. John Garnett introduced me as the District Secretary of the TGWU in the Oxford area, and the man largely responsible for the car industry.

'Oh indeed,' said His Royal Highness. 'So I suppose you're one of those people who always has the factories out on strike.'

Never one to let an opportunity slip, I replied, 'I think it's a reasonable assumption on my part that your Royal Highness has never worked on a car production line. Let me tell you about it,' and I proceeded to deliver a short description of life on the factory floor. He bore with me politely, and at the end he commented, 'Thank you. I am now much better informed than I was when this conversation began.'

Some time later the Queen also attended a function at our headquarters in Carlton House Terrace, and with her I had an informal and friendly chat; I found her much less hostile to my work in Industrial Relations.

The only other time I met the Queen was when I received my MBE. In November 1986 I had received a letter from Downing Street to say that I was to be offered this honour, and asking whether I would accept it. Since Margaret Thatcher was Prime Minister at the time, I was fairly sure that this was not intended as a reward for my trade union work. I tried to make discreet enquiries among a few contacts, and concluded eventually that the offer was based upon my work either for the Industrial Society or for the magistracy. While I was still debating whether to accept, Beryl offered her usual down-to-earth view. 'For heaven's sake don't be so stuck up about it, David. Just say thank you gracefully.' So I did.

Receiving it was great fun. Beryl and I and our two sons, Alan and Peter, set off for Buckingham Palace, feeling very important. I was soon cut down to size when we arrived. First of all I was separated from the family by someone who told us, 'Families this way, recipients that way.' The family were taken to the ballroom where the awards were to take place, and I was taken off to a very beautiful art gallery. There I found that areas had been roped off: one for ambassadors, another for peerages, another for knighthoods, and a fourth for ordinary mortals like me. There we all were, corralled like sheep in pens! Eventually we were led off to the ballroom, where I bowed, received my MBE, had a very brief chat with the Queen, and left. It was a most memorable and exciting day.

During the late 1970s I received several invitations to give talks about the work of the trade unions. Again, this was largely the result of the 'public profile' I was forced to develop during the industrial unrest at Cowley. One such invitation was from St George's House in Windsor Castle, which was being run as a study centre by the Deàn, Michael Mann. He was organising conferences and seminars on a wide range of subjects, with the common theme of current developments in society. In effect, these were designed to be a kind of sounding board to gather information for the Duke of Edinburgh and the Prince of Wales, who wished to be kept informed about developments in British society. I was invited to speak to a group of senior clergy on the role of trade unions, with specific reference to the problems of differentials between various groups within payment systems.

Giving a lecture in that forbidding library before those highly educated men was a most alarming experience for someone like myself who is not naturally articulate, who still bears the remnants of the old stammer, and who has had no formal education since the age of thirteen. Nevertheless I must have managed adequately because other invitations followed, and I returned to speak on the subject of problems in industry between unions and management. This was part of a series of discussions on all kinds of conflict in society, such as racial conflicts, religious conflicts, and women's rights. On this occasion the audience was a mixture of senior management, shop stewards, and trade union officials. On the day I attended, the final lecture was given by Michael Mann himself. In the course of his talk he referred to the problems caused by militant unions and trades unionists, who were causing havoc in industry and society. He said they should be removed because of the damage they were doing to the harmonious society he wished to see, by their constant calls for change.

To my great delight, when it came to question time a shop steward from the audience stood up and said,

'There was a man living two thousand years ago, who went around the Middle East causing trouble because he wanted changes in an unjust society. He preached a Sermon on the Mount about it. Would you describe Jesus Christ as a militant who ought to be removed?'

The Dean had no answer.

Another place I visited was St Peter's College, Radley, a local public school. The Warden of Radley College was Denis Silk, who was also a magistrate on the Abingdon bench, and he asked me to come and talk to the boys about trade unions in general. After one of my talks I was sitting in Hall having tea when a boy burst through the group with whom I was chatting and said angrily, 'People like you have to understand that this country is run by a meritocracy, and you and your kind will never be part of that meritocracy.' I turned to him and said, 'If you are stupid enough to make rude remarks like that, you won't be part of it either.' Not all the boys reacted like this, but there were always some who had a very 'them and us' outlook on life: they felt that they were definitely part of the privileged elite, while I as part of the working men's movement was clearly destined to be the underclass in their scheme of things.

I also went to another public school, Abingdon School, where I was warned that one of the boys was likely to interrupt my talk. Before I began, the headmaster, Sir James Cobban, told me that he had forbidden the boys to speak at all for the first twenty minutes of my talk. 'After that,' he said, 'you're on your own.' I thanked him and turned to the boys.

'As far as I'm concerned,' I said, 'you may feel quite free to interrupt and ask questions throughout this talk. I am used to addressing trade union branch meetings, not captive audiences.' This got a round of applause from them at once.

During the talk, as predicted, one boy stood up to interrupt. 'In my opinion, all trade unions should be banned everywhere,' he said.

'You will find that trade unions are banned in most fascist and communist countries,' I replied. 'Which of those two political persuasions do you belong to?' He promptly sat down, but the teacher called to him, 'As you have interrupted the speaker, you should answer his question.' He was extremely quiet after that.

At question time the head rose and said that he had a question for me.

'Mr Buckle, would you like to explain why there are up to nineteen unions in the car industry?' 'Certainly,' I answered. 'Provided that you will tell us afterwards why there are nine unions in the teaching profession, and which one you belong to.'

To do him justice, he not only delivered his answer, but added that on the following weekend he would be attending the Headmasters' Conference in Scarborough.

'So we have one thing in common, Headmaster,' I replied. 'We are both trade unionists, and you are going to your trade union conference this weekend.' The boys loved it.

A more recent visit to Radley College was for an informal 'Any Questions' session. The panel was chaired by Sir Robin Day (who had a son at the school at the time), and included Norman Stone (a right-wing historian), the Warden, Denis Silk, and myself. The date was 20th November 1990, Mrs Thatcher was in Paris, and as we gathered for dinner at Denis Silk's house before the meeting, we knew that the leadership election for the Conservative Party was taking place. The evening news bulletin carried the announcement that Mrs Thatcher had lost by a small margin, and so Sir Robin insisted that the TV was brought into the dining room during dinner. Throughout the meal he kept shouting at the Warden to switch channels to follow one news report after another, and treated us all to a running commentary on the quality of every reporter. It made normal conversation quite impossible, and it was clear to all of us that on such an important night he would rather be anywhere else but Radley.

Eventually we went in to the meeting, and Sir Robin's first question to the panel was an invitation to comment on the events of the day and to say what we thought of the future prospects of the Prime Minister. It presented me with a golden opportunity to say exactly what I thought about Thatcherism!

I have been a parish councillor in Radley village since 1951, because this is a contribution I can make to the local life of my village; Beryl and I still live in the council house into which we moved with Eve and our two sons in 1950. When I retired from full-time work in 1988 I took about six months' rest, but then the Oxford Labour Party asked me to stand as County Councillor for one of the Oxford wards. I was selected for the Wood Farm ward and was elected in 1989. Once a member of the County Council I gradually became more and more busy: I nominated as my special interest the department of Leisure and Arts, but of course I took an interest in all the other work too. I was elected Chair of the Labour Group on the Council and then Deputy Leader. For some years Oxfordshire has been a hung council, with no political party having overall control, and so the main parties take it in turns to take the chair. In 1996 it was the turn of the Labour Group, and I was nominated and elected as Chair of the County Council (in 1997 I was unanimously re-elected Chair for a further year).

It was a very busy and intensive year: I attended 360 official engagements and nearly 100 semi-official ones; I chaired every council meeting; I attended most major programme committees, and spent at least six hours a week on administration. During the difficult and protracted discussions over setting the County budget I needed all my negotiating skills, but I was fascinated by the whole process. Once again I felt that I was doing a real and useful job on behalf of ordinary people, and by listening fairly and impartially to all parties I was able to encourage them along to reach an equitable agreement.

A particular joy that year was meeting Nelson Mandela in person when he came to Oxford to speak at the Sheldonian Theatre. Afterwards a dinner was held in his honour in Wadham College, and as Chair of the Council I was seated at the top table opposite him and the Prince of Wales; for the first time I was delighted to have achieved a status that enabled me to be there. I had long admired this great man who has suffered so much and has somehow led his country from oppression to democracy without bitterness or bloodshed. I showed him a badge, beautifully produced in the ANC colours and bearing his profile, which the TUC had produced at their congress in 1988, to celebrate his seventieth birthday. He examined it carefully, and said that he had heard about it but had never seen one; he asked if he might keep it as a souvenir of his visit to Oxford. He was the only person I was happy to pass it on to.

One tradition in Oxfordshire is that an official photograph is taken of each Chairperson, and hung in a sort of Rogue's Gallery along a certain corridor. My picture hangs opposite that of Lady Parker, the daughter of Lord Macclesfield, who himself was Chair of the County Council for no less than thirty years. When I look at that picture I can see not only how far I have come in my lifetime, but how far local democracy has moved on. No longer can one person hold office simply by virtue of his status at birth, nor hold on to office without challenge for such a long period.

Many years ago I met Lord Macclesfield in the course of my work as a trade unionist, when I was jointly chairing a meeting with him. When he left the room everyone else stood up, and he overheard me saying to the other members that it was not necessary to stand as a mark of respect for him. I followed him outside and explained that I meant no special disrespect to him, but that I was not in the habit of standing when I met with the management. He growled at me, 'It's not my favourite pastime, meeting with trade union officials like you.' I replied, 'And it's not my favourite pastime to meet with peers of the realm.'

It gives me enormous satisfaction to see my photograph up there in the corridor with his, a man of equal standing in spite of the difference in our birth and education, with my service to the community applauded as much as his.

I am more than content with what I have achieved, against all the odds and against all my expectation. I have been blessed with a loving and loyal wife, two splendid sons, and four lovely grandchildren, Kate, Nicholas, Rhianna and Tom. On 30th December 1994 we celebrated our Golden Wedding Anniversary, and our sons arranged a wonderful party with over a hundred guests, both family and friends. To someone such as me with no early experience of family life to draw on, their love and support seem a miracle. It has sustained me and guided me in all my work.

I hope that I have been able to do some good. Through my work as a shop steward and a trade unionist I have been able to help people both at an individual level with their own problems and on a broader level with improvements to pay and working conditions that have helped hundreds of working people. I have done my best as a magistrate to temper justice with mercy and common sense, and I have tried to represent the best interests of local people through my work as a Councillor.

I don't really feel that my life has been one of 'Hostilities Only', yet it is an apt phrase to describe so many of my formative experiences. Looking back, it seems to me that I have been incredibly fortunate. The home where I began my life, a pathetic scrap of skinny childhood, unwanted and unloved, poorly fed and poorly educated, was truly a hostile environment for a child. My wartime experience, though mercifully quiet, taught me some useful lessons, labelled as I was by the Marines as one of their members 'for Hostilities Only'. In my later service in industry I was sometimes accused of looking for trouble – by both sides! – but in fact I never sought out hostilities; I merely faced up to situations as they arose. On the other hand, I never ran away from a scrap, and as a magistrate and a Councillor I continued to stand up for justice and the rights of the working people wherever possible.

My commitment to my working-class roots has never altered. I still believe that it is the right of every working person not to be exploited or treated unfairly, and that we should keep on fighting those hostilities of injustice and exploitation wherever we find them.

Printed by Leach's.the Printers
54 Ock Street, Abingdon OX14 5DE
Tel: 01235 520444